MONOGRAPHS OF THE SOCIETY FOR RESEARCH IN CHILD DEVELOPMENT

SERIAL NO. 214, VOL. 51, NO. 3

INFANT SEARCH AND OBJECT PERMANENCE: A META-ANALYSIS OF THE A-NOT-B ERROR

HENRY M. WELLMAN
UNIVERSITY OF MICHIGAN

DAVID CROSS
TEXAS CHRISTIAN UNIVERSITY

KAREN BARTSCH
UNIVERSITY OF MICHIGAN

WITH COMMENTARY BY
PAUL L. HARRIS

AND REPLY BY THE AUTHORS

MONOGRAPHS OF THE SOCIETY FOR RESEARCH IN CHILD
DEVELOPMENT, SERIAL NO. 214, VOL. 51, NO. 3

CONTENTS

ABSTRACT   V

I. INTRODUCTION   1

II. METHOD   6

III. RESULTS   11

IV. DISCUSSION   30

V. CONCLUSIONS   46

REFERENCES   47

ACKNOWLEDGMENTS   51

BRINGING ORDER TO THE A-NOT-B ERROR:
COMMENTARY BY PAUL L. HARRIS   52
MORE DATA, MORE THEORY, AND MORE ORDER:
REPLY BY THE AUTHORS   62

NEW EDITOR

We are pleased to announce that, as of July 1, 1987, Wanda Bronson will succeed Robert N. Emde as editor of the Monographs of the Society for Research in Child Development. Please send future submissions to

Wanda Bronson
Institute of Human Development
Tolman Hall
University of California, Berkeley
Berkeley, CA 94720

ABSTRACT

WELLMAN, HENRY M.; CROSS, DAVID; and BARTSCH, KAREN. Infant Search and Object Permanence: A Meta-Analysis of the A-Not-B Error. With Commentary by PAUL L. HARRIS; WITH Reply by HENRY M. WELLMAN, DAVID CROSS, and KAREN BARTSCH. *Monographs of the Society for Research in Child Development*, 1986, **51**(3, Serial No. 214).

Research on Piaget's stage 4 object concept has failed to reveal a clear or consistent pattern of results. Piaget found that 8–12-month-old infants would make perseverative errors; his explanation for this phenomenon was that the infant's concept of the object was contextually dependent on his or her actions. Some studies designed to test Piaget's explanation have replicated Piaget's basic finding, yet many have found no preference for the A location or the B location or an actual preference for the B location. More recently, researchers have attempted to uncover the causes for these results concerning the A-not-B error. Again, however, different studies have yielded different results, and qualitative reviews have failed to yield a consistent explanation for the results of the individual studies. This state of affairs suggests that the phenomenon may simply be too complex to be captured by individual studies varying 1 factor at a time and by reviews based on similar qualitative considerations. Therefore, the current investigation undertook a meta-analysis, a synthesis capturing the quantitative information across the now sizable number of studies.

We entered several important factors into the meta-analysis, including the effects of age, the number of A trials, the length of delay between hiding and search, the number of locations, the distances between locations, and the distinctive visual properties of the hiding arrays. Of these, the analysis consistently indicated that age, delay, and number of hiding locations strongly influence infants' search. The pattern of specific findings also yielded new information about infant search. A general characterization of the results is that, at every age, both above-chance and below-chance performance was observed. That is, at each age at least 1 combination of delay and number of locations yielded above-chance A-not-B errors or significant perseverative search. At the same time, at each age at least 1 alternative combination of delay and number of locations yielded below-chance errors and significant above-chance correct performance, that is, significantly accurate search. These 2 findings, appropriately elaborated, allow us to evaluate all extant theories of stage 4 infant search. When this is done, all these extant accounts prove to be incorrect. That is, they are incommensurate with one aspect or another of the pooled findings in the meta-analysis. Therefore, we end by proposing a new account that is consistent with the entire data set.

I. INTRODUCTION

Object permanence is an important theoretical construct. It is also a topic that has been widely researched with infants. Object permanence refers to an organism's implicit knowledge that objects exist independent of one's own actions and visual contact and that they coexist with the self in a larger space containing both. Given such knowledge, someone who sees an object disappear behind a visual screen believes that the object continues to exist even though it is no longer visible. The theoretical importance of such an understanding is clear: imagine the worldview and actions of an organism without it. Such an organism "lives in an ever-changing world where objects are continually made and unmade" (Harris, 1983, p. 716). Whether infants possess basically correct notions of the permanence of objects and how such notions develop are thus issues of considerable importance.

Piaget (1954) addressed these issues, and his is the classic account. Piaget believed that object permanence was central to an understanding of space, time, and causality and, yet, that a conception of permanent, spatially coexisting objects developed rather late in infancy. Young infants were like the deficient organism described above. For at least two reasons, Piaget's claims have been the subject of considerable research. He made apparent the fundamental importance of object permanence, and he attributed to young infants a large and tantalizing conceptual deficiency.

Piaget's is a developmental account in which the infant's understanding of object permanence evolves and matures over six stages from birth to approximately 18 months. Nevertheless, a particularly important part of Piaget's theory concerns the behavior and notions of stage 4 infants. At about 8–10 months, or at stage 4, infants begin to search for hidden objects. Before this time, if an object is completely hidden from view, the child does not search for it no matter how much he desires it. For Piaget, lack of such search in younger infants is an important piece of evidence that, before they reach stage 4, infants do not conceive of independent, spatially localized objects. Indeed, even the stage 4 infant does not do so. While stage 4 infants will search for hidden objects, they still exhibit a particularly informative error. If an object is first hidden and found in one of several locations (the A location) and then hidden in a second location (the B location), the infant proceeds to search for the object in the original A location. This is the A-not-B, or perseverative, error. The error occurs, it is claimed, even though the B hiding is performed in clear view of the infant, who carefully attends to it and clearly wants the hidden item. The error has been the focus of considerable attention by Piaget and others.

For Piaget this provocative error is particularly revealing. Its occurrence suggests that, even at this relatively late age, the stage 4 infant does not really or fully conceive of an external independent object out there in space. Piaget's explanation of the perseverative error is rich, extended, and in places contradictory. It is therefore difficult to summarize accurately. Nonetheless, two aspects of Piaget's interpretation are clear. First, the perseverative error is interpreted as revealing a continuation in stage 4 infants of the same problems with object permanence obvious in still younger infants. Second, in a strict sense it is incorrect to say that the infant "searches" for "objects." Instead, it would be more accurate to say that the infant has simply learned an action (searching at A) that creates the object for him rather than localizing it in space. When the object again disappears (at B), the child's actions are not really attempts to retrieve the temporarily invisible object but rather attempts to re-create it. Thus, the infant "searches" at A or, more correctly, performs once again the action that created the object in his or her prior experience. Note that there are two critical aspects of this "search" behavior (Harris, 1987). The infant does not understand that objects continue to exist spatially when out of sight. Objects are not hidden from view and uncovered; they are made and unmade. Further, the infant believes that *his* actions make and unmake the object. In total, "the act of finding a displaced image would be confused, in the subject's consciousness, with the act of recreating it" (Piaget, 1954, p. 103).

The presence of the A-not-B error at this late age is specially important because it supports (a) Piaget's interpretation of earlier behavior as well as (b) his use of search tasks as an index of object concepts and especially object permanence. At earlier ages the infant can retrieve partially hidden objects, can track objects as they move across his field of vision, and will even look for objects that have just dropped out of sight around him (Piaget, 1954). These behaviors might suggest some early appreciation of objects' permanence. However, to the extent that the subsequent appearance of A-not-B errors shows lack of such permanence in 9-month-old infants, it substantiates Piaget's interpretation that still earlier behaviors do not indicate object permanence. Relatedly, it is certainly possible that infants may have a mature object concept but simply not have acquired the behaviors necessary to reveal it on search tasks (reaching, lifting the obstruction, retrieving the object). That is, the stage 3 infant, who fails to search for hidden objects, may simply be evidencing motor rather than conceptual difficulties. Against this possibility, however, is the fact that, even at stage 4, when children clearly can search (e.g., they retrieve hidden objects on the A trials of the stage 4 task), they still make the revealing A-not-B error. The A-not-B error shows that the conceptual difficulty is still present at a point at which the prerequisite search skills are well developed.

A considerable body of research has accumulated, focusing on and attempting to explain the A-not-B error. Several different reasons together motivate this research. There is the provocative nature of the error—that infants make such a counterintuitive mistake at all provokes attempts to explain it. There is also the importance of the error in Piaget's account and to an understanding of object permanence. More recently, there is the existence of considerable inconsistency in empirical findings pertaining to the error. For example, some researchers report finding A-not-B errors occurring at levels above chance (e.g., Butterworth, 1977; Landers, 1971; Piaget, 1954), some report finding below-chance levels of these errors (e.g., Gratch, Appel, Evans, LeCompte, & Wright, 1974; Harris, 1973), and still others have found perseverative errors occurring at about chance levels (e.g., Butterworth, 1977; Evans, 1973). Hence, there is doubt, first, about whether the A-not-B error is a replicable phenomenon and, second, if it is replicable, about the conditions necessary for its appearance.

The magnitude of this research literature and its apparent discrepancies mandate a careful review. Indeed, several qualitative reviews have been presented (e.g., Bremner, 1985; Cornell, 1978; Gratch, 1975; Harris, 1983, 1987; Moore & Meltzoff, 1978; Wellman & Somerville, 1982). The current endeavor is an attempt to provide a quantitative review and integration of the findings: a meta-analysis.

Several aspects of the existing situation make a meta-analysis seem particularly useful. First, the different qualitative reviews have come to quite different interpretations of the existing research. Second, several of the discrepancies involved can be addressed by meta-analysis. Thus, for example, if studies show a mixture of above-, at-, and below-chance responding, then a pooling of the data across studies is needed to establish the existence of the phenomena at all. Third, the number of studies is large enough to provide sample sizes sufficient for meta-analysis. Finally, the nature of the data is especially amenable to meta-analysis. The essential measures involved are proportions—for example, the number of infants out of those tested who make the error. A meta-analysis of such data is especially straightforward; many of the statistical problems that arise for other sorts of meta-analyses, which require the transformation and collapsing of various derived inferential statistics (F tests, t tests, etc.) across studies (see Glass, McGaw, & Smith, 1981), can be avoided given this sort of data.

The considerations above essentially concern the nature of the dependent variable—the A-not-B error as reported across studies. Of equal importance are possible independent variables, such as the age of the children tested. Investigations of the perseverative error have differed widely according to the independent variables included in their designs. This variety of independent variables has contributed to a confused picture of infant performance. However, the situation is again amenable to meta-analysis. Sufficient variation exists on a number of independent variables—including the number of A trials (e.g., Evans, 1973), the length of the delay between hiding and search (e.g., Harris, 1973), and more recently the inclusion of more than two locations (e.g., Cummings & Bjork, 1983a, 1983b)—so that these can be used in quantitative analyses of the dependent variable. Indeed, in this regard a meta-analysis should prove especially informative. Variation across studies allows examination of factors that were not comprehensively varied within studies since studies typically include a single value on most of these variables.

Four independent variables deserve brief introduction since they figure prominently in prior studies, in current theoretical discussions, and in the following analyses. The first is age. According to Piaget (1954), perseverative responding is prototypical of stage 4 only and thus should vary with age. Indeed, on the basis of longitudinal studies it seems likely that perseverative responding occurs only early in the stage 4 period (e.g., Gratch & Landers, 1971). The second is the number of A trials the child receives before the object is hidden at B. In Piaget's account the child's prior experiences at A shape him to believe that the object can be re-created by uncovering A, even when the object was hidden at B. Thus, variation in the number of A trials should be intimately related to the strength and nature of A-not-B errors. Equally important is the delay between when the object is hidden at B and when the infant is first allowed to search. Several investigators (Gratch et al., 1974; Harris, 1973) have found that A-not-B errors do not occur unless some delay is instituted; when infants search immediately on the object's disappearance at B, they search correctly. Finally, there is the number of locations available to the infant for search. The traditional test situation has two such locations. Recently, more locations have been included (e.g., Cummings & Bjork, 1983a, 1983b; Sophian & Wellman, 1983). Cummings and Bjork, for example, noted that the appearance of the A-not-B error may simply be an artifact of the two-location test since in that situation if infants search erroneously for any reason they must search at A. Several other less prominent variables will be described as they are introduced into the analysis.

A meta-analysis must be guided by an organized set of questions and hypotheses that it addresses. We have attempted to evaluate extant theoretical perspectives against the data and to originate a new perspective where necessary. Our analysis was originally aimed at evaluating four general models of infants' search.

1. The simplest of these is a model proposing *random search,* which predicts that infants will search randomly, displaying neither significant perseveration to the A location nor significantly correct search at the B location. This model provides the null hypothesis against which other models are tested.

2. The second is a *perseverative search* model, which predicts that, to the extent that infant search differs from random search, it will tend toward the A location. This model corresponds in essence to Piaget's (1954) hypotheses about the search of stage 4 infants.

3. The third model is a *correct search* model, predicting that infant search, when nonrandom, will tend toward the B location. This model corresponds to, for example, Cummings and Bjork's (1983a, 1983b) hypotheses about infant search.

4. A fourth possibility is a *combined components* model. Such a model incorporates both perseverative and correct tendencies.

II. METHOD

Meta-analytic procedures are available for (a) combining results from studies in which experimental groups are compared with a control group and (b) combining results to investigate the effects of one or more independent variables on the dependent variable of interest (Glass et al., 1981). The latter case is our concern. In a meta-analysis, conditions within studies, rather than individual subjects or entire studies, compose the units of analysis (Glass et al., 1981). In our research, we have used the proportion of infants in a condition who demonstrate the target behaviors—A-not-B errors or correct search at B—as the dependent variable. The details of our analytic methods will be presented in Chapter III. Here, we describe the studies and conditions included in the analysis.

The potentially relevant literature is extensive. In addition to Piaget's view, researchers have proposed that the A-not-B error is a memory problem, a motor or habit phenomenon, and an information-processing problem, to name just a few variations. These views have spawned many different investigations.

We began by searching this literature for studies on a variety of related topics—for example, object permanence, the A-not-B error, perseveration, the object concept, infant or toddler search, and spatial representation. We depended for references primarily on several qualitative reviews of this research (Bremner, 1985; Cornell, 1978; Gratch, 1975; Harris, 1983, 1987; Moore & Meltzoff, 1978; Sophian, 1984; and Wellman, 1985). The relevant studies referred to in each review were sought, as were the references in each of those studies, until the lists were exhausted. This set of studies was supplemented by a search of *Psychological Abstracts* (exhaustively for the years 1975–84, less thoroughly before that) and by personal communications with several of the researchers in the field (L. P. Acredolo, J. G. Bremner, A. Diamond, P. L. Harris, and C. Sophian). The final set of studies includes both published and unpublished works. Several unpublished works (e.g., Appel, 1971; Landers, 1968; Moore, 1973) were not obtained; nevertheless, we considered almost all the published material available on the topic of the A-not-B error and a large sample of unpublished work as well.

The meta-analysis was conducted on several subsamples of this accumulated set of studies. For both pragmatic and more conceptual reasons, not all the collected studies and conditions could be included. Consider first the pragmatic difficulties.

Meta-analyses of the sort we undertook require comparably reported data on the dependent measure across studies—the A-not-B error. The most commonly reported measure of the A-not-B error was the error made on the first B trial. Fortunately, this is also the most theoretically relevant measure. In our final analyses, only conditions reporting A-not-B errors for the first B trial were used.

Several types of studies failed to meet this minimum criterion. One group was composed of studies that provided only one location of search (e.g., Dunst, Brooks, & Doxsey, 1982; Gratch, 1972; Harris, 1971; Kramer, Hill, & Cohen, 1975; Rader, Spiro, & Firestone, 1979) and thus could not measure an A-not-B search error. A second group was composed of those studies that did not measure manual search errors at all but reported some other dependent measure—for example, the infant's anticipation of the object's presence, absence, or movement via visual tracking of the object or movements of the head (e.g., Acredolo, 1978; Acredolo & Evans, 1980; Presson & Ihrig, 1982; Reiser, 1979) or the infant's surprise or puzzlement (e.g., LeCompte & Gratch, 1972; Meicler & Gratch, 1980), fixation (e.g., Willatts, 1979), or persistence of search (e.g., Harris, 1971). A third group included studies that did not provide a clearly reported measure of first-B-trial performance even though they studied perseverative search (e.g., Neilson, 1982, who reported an error measure collapsed over a number of trials so that there was no first-B-trial information). Finally, longitudinal studies were not amenable to our meta-analysis. In longitudinal studies the dependent variable was almost invariably the average age at which a group of children succeeded on a particular hiding task (e.g., Bower & Patterson, 1972; Gratch & Landers, 1971; Kramer et al., 1975; Miller, Cohen, & Hill, 1970) rather than the amount of A-not-B errors made by a group of children at a certain age.

As noted in Chapter I, different studies have included a wide variety of different search conditions. A great many of these were reasonably comparable or differed only in relevant measurable ways (e.g., numbers of locations, delay, etc.). Some, however, were so different in method as to be incompatible with the larger group. For example, Harris (1974) reported conditions in which the children searched at a locked door. Since the child could not actually retrieve the object, this study was excluded. Similarly, conditions in which there was no toy hidden (e.g., Appel & Gratch, 1984) or

TABLE 1

Number Key for Studies and Conditions

Study Designation Numbers	Condition Designation Letters	Condition Descriptions
1. Appel & Gratch (1984)	a	9 months; toy-toy condition
	b	12 months; toy-toy condition
2. Bjork & Cummings (1984, Experiment 1)	a	5 locations
3. Bjork & Cummings (1984, Experiment 2)	a	2 locations
	b	5 locations
4. Bremner & Bryant (1977)	a	Traditional; distinctive backgrounds
5. Bremner (1978)	a	Traditional: distinctive covers
6. Butterworth (1975, Experiment 1)	a	A midline; B periphery
	b	B midline; A periphery
7. Butterworth (1975, Experiment 2)	a	A midline; B periphery
	b	B midline; A periphery
8. Butterworth (1976)	a	8 months; A lower
	b	9 months; A lower
	c	10 months; A lower
	d	8 months; A upper
	e	9 months; A upper
	f	10 months; A upper
9. Butterworth (1977)	a	8 months; 3 A trials; traditional
	b	8 months; 5 A trials; traditional
	c	9 months; 3 A trials; traditional
	d	9 months; 5 A trials; traditional
	e	10 months; 3 A trials; traditional
10. Butterworth & Jarrett (1982, Experiment 3)	a	1 A trial; 8 months
	b	1 A trial; 9 months
	c	1 A trial; 10 months
	d	5 A trials; 8 months
	e	5 A trials; 9 months
	f	5 A trials; 10 months
11. Butterworth, Jarrett, & Hicks (1982, Experiment I)	a	Condition II; 8 months
	b	Condition II; 9 months
	c	Condition II; 10 months
	d	Condition III; 8 months
	e	Condition III; 9 months
	f	Condition III; 10 months
	g	Condition IV; 8 months
	h	Condition IV; 9 months
	i	Condition IV; 10 months
12. Butterworth, Jarrett, & Hicks (1982, Experiment II)	a	Condition I; 8 months
	b	Condition I; 9 months
	c	Condition I; 10 months
13. Cummings & Bjork (1983a) ...	a	5 locations; end-middle
	b	5 locations; end-end
	c	5 locations; middle-end

8

TABLE 1 (*Continued*)

Study Designation Numbers	Condition Designation Letters	Condition Descriptions
14. Cummings & Bjork (1983b) ...	a	3 locations
	b	5 locations
	c	6 locations
15. Evans (1973)	a	2 A trials; passive experience
	b	2 A trials; active experience
	c	5 A trials; passive experience
	d	5 A trials; active experience
16. Evans & Gratch (1972)	a	Same toy
17. Frye (1980, Experiment I)	a	Control
	b	Distraction
	c	Partial hiding
18. Frye (1980, Experiment II) ...	a	Partial hiding
19. Gratch, Appel, Evans, LeCompte, & Wright (1974) ...	a	0-sec delay
	b	1-sec delay
	c	3-sec delay
	d	7-sec delay
	e	0-sec delay
20. Harris (1973, Experiment I) ...	a	Change location; same response
21. Harris (1973, Experiment II) ..	a	0-sec delay
	b	5-sec delay
22. Harris (1973, Experiment III)	a	Condition "1"
	b	Condition "2"
23. Horobin & Acredolo (1986) ...	a	2 location; narrow distance
	b	2 location; wide distance
	c	6 location
24. Landers (1971)	a	Little active experience
	b	Much active experience
	c	Passive experience
25. Schuberth, Werner, & Lipsitt (1978)	a	Same toy
26. Sophian (1985)	a	2 locations; traditional
	b	3 locations; traditional
27. Sophian & Sage (1985)	a	9 months
	b	16 months
28. Sophian & Wellman (1983, Experiment I)	a	9 months; visible hiding
	b	9 months; finding at A
	c	9 months; 1 trial at A
	d	9 months; 3 trials at A
	e	16 months; visible hiding
	f	16 months; finding at A
	g	16 months; 1 trial at A
	h	16 months; 3 trials at A
29. Sophian & Yengo (1985)	a	Hidden object; 2 locations
	b	Hidden object; 3 locations
30. Webb, Massar, & Nadolny (1972, 16 months)	a	Cups
	b	Toy chest
	c	Quart container

in which the toy was changed for a new toy between A and B trials (e.g., Evans & Gratch, 1972; Schuberth, Werner, & Lipsitt, 1978) were excluded. In these cases it is not clear what the child was searching for or whether A and B trials have the traditional interpretation. Similarly, conditions in which the object was visible when "hidden" (e.g., by being hidden under transparent covers) were excluded (Bremner & Knowles, 1984; Butterworth, 1977; Harris, 1974; Neilson, 1982; Sophian & Yengo, 1985).[1]

Two other exclusions were made. First, the few conditions in which a person rather than an object was hidden were excluded (Bell, 1970; Corter, Zucker, & Galligan, 1980; Paradise & Curcio, 1974). Jackson, Campos, and Fischer (1978) have shown that, when comparably conducted, hiding an object and hiding a person (even the infant's mother) yield comparable findings. However, studies of person permanence do not typically use comparably controlled conditions (with the exception of the Jackson et al. study, which, unfortunately for our purposes, was conducted and reported longitudinally). Finally, conditions in which the infants or the hiding array was rotated or moved between A and B trials (e.g., Bremner & Bryant, 1977) were excluded. Pragmatically, it was not clear for our purposes how the infants' responses in such a situation (although often informative) should be coded. Specifically, in these cases it is unclear which location is the B location since one location is the B location in an absolute sense and the other location is the B location in relation to the infant's position. Rather than arbitrarily assuming that one of these definitions is best and defining the A-not-B error on that basis, we excluded such studies from the meta-analysis.

Since whether a condition met the criteria above was not always clear cut, all conditions were judged by two independent raters blind to each other's choices. No disagreements occurred as to the inclusion or exclusion of any conditions; hence, interrater reliability was 100%.

It should be noted that in most cases only some conditions in a study were excluded; the other conditions met the relevant criteria. Thus, the meta-analysis is largely representative of the studies in the field (with the single exception of longitudinal research studies). Moreover, a great number of conditions met these criteria; 89 conditions from 30 studies are included in the formal analyses. A list of these studies and conditions is presented in Table 1 and will be detailed further in what follows. Finally, if the above restrictions had not been adopted, a meta-analysis would have been largely uninterpretable when, for example, results emerged from an analysis collapsing together standard tasks, visible hidings, rotated hidings, substituted objects, and locked doors.

---

[1] However, these studies are discussed in the expanded version of this *Monograph*, which is available from the authors.

III. RESULTS

STANDARD TWO-LOCATION ANALYSES

We first examined the effects of three key independent variables—infant age, number of A trials, and length of delay between hiding and finding—on the proportion of infants in an experimental condition who exhibit the A-not-B error. An additional variable—year of publication—was also included. Though this variable is of no current theoretical interest, examining the year of publication provides an important control in meta-analyses (Green & Hall, 1984). Initially, we included only what we term "standard two-location tasks," that is, only those conditions that had identical location covers and backgrounds, involved the same object throughout the task, had two horizontally oriented hiding locations, and involved hiding the object at one location (A) on A trials and then hiding it at the other location (B) for the focal B trial. There were a total of 34 conditions within our sample that satisfied these criteria. The frequency breakdown for these conditions is shown in Table 2.

Our analysis here and in later sections involved three steps. First, linear regressions were used to screen for significant main effects and all possible two-variable interactions. Higher-order interactions were not investigated because the cells in the design were too sparse (see Table 2). Second, we tested the four search models outlined in Chapter I. To do so, we used a linear model that retained only those variables shown to have a significant effect in step 1. We constructed confidence bands around the obtained regression line or plane and then determined if these bands included the A-not-B error values hypothesized by the random search model. If the values hypothesized by the random search model lie within such confidence bands, then the data are consistent with random search; if they do not, then one of the other search models must be considered.

Third, we supplemented these analyses by using bootstrap methods. Glass et al. (1981) warn against relying too heavily on ordinary least squares when the data do not have the usual sampling properties found in ordinary

TABLE 2

Number of Conditions and Study Identification Numbers
for the Standard Two-Location Analyses

	Delay (Sec)				
Age (Months)	0	1–2	3	5–7	Total
8.0–8.9	0	2	4	1	7
9.0–9.9	3	5	12	2	22
10.0–11.9	1	0	4	0	5
Total	4	7	20	3	34
	Number of A Trials				
	1	2	3	4–8	Total
8.0–8.9	1	1	2	3	7
9.0–9.9	2	4	5	11	22
10.0–11.9	1	0	2	2	5
Total	4	5	9	16	34

NOTE.—Study identification numbers, as listed in Table 1, are 1a–b, 3a, 9a–f, 11d–f, 15a–d, 16a, 17a, 19a–e, 20a, 21a–b, 23a–b, 24a–c, 25a, 26a, and 29a. The *mean* ages of infants in each condition as cited in the original reports have been used to construct this table and for analyses using age as a variable. The mean ages for the various conditions range as noted in the stub column.

research. In particular, since several conditions are often taken from a single study, the observations in a meta-analysis can have dependencies not found when observations are made on individuals. These dependencies can be incorporated into bootstrap analyses (Efron, 1982; Efron & Gong, 1983).

Regression analysis.—Bivariate plots of the dependent variable—the proportion of infants making the A-not-B error—against each of the independent variables—age, A trials, delay, and year of publication—revealed a curvilinear relation between errors and delay. Increasing delay systematically led to increased errors, but this relation tapered off at longer delays. Consequently, delay was transformed for subsequent analyses using the transformation ln(delay + 1) (Draper & Smith, 1981). In addition, the dependent variable, which is a proportion score, was transformed using the arcsine transformation in order to stabilize the error variances (Snedecor & Cochran, 1980).[2]

[2] The analyses in this meta-analysis using transformed variables have been replicated using the untransformed versions. Transforming the independent variables so as to account for the nonlinear relation between them (e.g., age and delay in the current analysis) makes no difference in the substantive outcomes of the analyses. The sole difference is that the regression between the independent variables and infant errors is stronger using the transformed versions, which is reflected in higher R^2 values. This is as it should be because, if the relation is in fact nonlinear and the transformed version of the independent variable

The Pearson product-moment correlations between the five variables—year, age, A trials, delay, and perseverative errors—yielded only two significant correlations ($p < .01$).[3] There was a substantial negative correlation between age and perseverative errors ($r = -.49$), indicating that the proportion of A-not-B errors decreases as the average age for a condition increases. There was a substantial positive correlation between delay and errors ($r = .56$), indicating that the proportion of A-not-B errors increases as the delay between hiding and searching increases.

The stepwise regression of perseverative errors on the four independent variables yielded a total sum of squares of 222, of which 120 were accounted for by the independent variables. The regression algorithm entered at each step the variable that would lead to the largest reduction in the residual sum of squares. Delay and age were the important variables in the regression, accounting for 69 and 50 of the 120 regression sum of squares, respectively. A trials and year contribute little (sums of squares are one and zero, respectively). The F ratios for delay and age, respectively, are $F(1,32) = 14.43$, $p < .001$, and $F(1,31) = 15.05$, $p < .001$; for A trials and year, $F < 1$.[4]

A further test was made to determine if any of the two-variable interaction terms would contribute beyond the main effects. In every case the contribution of the interaction was nonsignificant, $F < 1$, indicating that the main effects were sufficient to model the relation between errors, on the one hand, and age and delay, on the other. If only delay and age are used in the linear model for perseverative errors, $R^2 = .54$, and the following coefficients are obtained (with standard errors in parentheses):

$$\text{perseverative errors} = 8.8 - 1.8[\text{age}] + 2.7[\text{delay}]. \qquad (1a)$$
$$\phantom{\text{perseverative errors} = } (1.3) \quad (0.5) \qquad (0.6)$$

---

accounts for this, then there should be a better fit of the model to the data. We report the analyses employing transformed variables because these results more accurately reflect the effects of age, delay, and number of locations on infant searching for the type of modeling we are conducting. In addition, no patterns of extreme curvilinearity were observed (e.g., U- or S-shaped functions); rather logarithmic patterns were. With logarithmic patterns the inherent nature of the relation—monotonic increase or decrease in one variable as a function of the other—is not changed by the transformation.

[3] The usual tests of significance are not necessarily appropriate for meta-analyses because conditions are not independent (see Glass et al., 1981). We have compensated in two ways. First, we tend toward the conservative whenever we present significance levels. Thus, we adopt the .01 rather than the .05 level of significance for evaluating correlations. Second, we have supplemented all our primary analyses with bootstrapped analyses.

[4] An alternate statistic that provides nonredundant information involves t ratios from the full regression. The F ratios are dependent on the order of entry of the variables, whereas the t ratios are calculated once all the variables have been entered and are hence independent of their order of entry. In this analysis, and in all the subsequent analyses, the stepwise F tests and the full regression t tests lead to identical conclusions.

Outlier analysis.—Analysis of residuals was used to check the assumptions of the linear model. Well-known graphic techniques were used to check normality (from a histogram of the residuals), homoscedasticity (from a plot of the residuals against the predicted values), and linearity (from plots of the dependent variable against the independent variables) (Draper & Smith, 1981). Graphing the residuals also allows the detection of outliers in the sample. In the current analysis (and all the following analyses as well), the assumptions of normality, homoscedasticity, and linearity were satisfied. However, the residual analysis did uncover an outlier, a single data point separated from the other data points that clustered together. This point corresponded to condition 23b (see Table 1), Horobin and Acredolo's (1986) wide-pair condition—a condition in which the distance between the two hiding locations was great. Two statistics support the graphic analysis. First, the unit normal deviate form (Draper & Smith, 1981) of the residual is -2.83. In this standardized form, over 99% of the residuals should lie between -2.6 and 2.6. Second, the outlying residual can be tested using a t statistic (Snedecor & Cochran, 1980), $t(30) = -3.35, p = .003$.

This outlying condition does not distort the nature of our general pattern of results; essentially, it affects the analyses by adding noise, that is, by inflating the mean square error of the regression. Thus, when condition 23b is deleted from the data set, R^2 increases from .54 to .62, and the linear model is

$$\text{errors} = 8.7 - 1.7[\text{age}] + 2.9[\text{delay}]. \tag{1b}$$
$$(1.1) \quad (0.4) \quad (0.5)$$

There is little difference between the coefficients in equations (1a) and (1b).

Confidence bands.—An informative method for presenting the results is to use confidence bands around the regression plane obtained from regressing errors on age and delay. A slice of one such band is shown in Figure 1, which presents the effect of delay on A-not-B errors for 9-month-old infants. These confidence bands are natural extensions of confidence intervals for the population mean, with the exception that confidence limits are formed for the conditional mean of the dependent variable at different combinations of the independent variables. These are simultaneous confidence bands that contain the error rate at .05 no matter how many combinations of the independent variables are investigated (Draper & Smith, 1981). The central question for our purpose is, Are the values predicted by the random search model contained within the confidence band? In Figure 1, the proportion of A-not-B errors predicted by the random search model (i.e., .50) is contained within the band for a delay of 1 sec but lies above the band for a delay of 0 sec and below the band for delays of 3 or 5 sec. Hence, at shorter delays, 9-month-old infants are making fewer errors than would

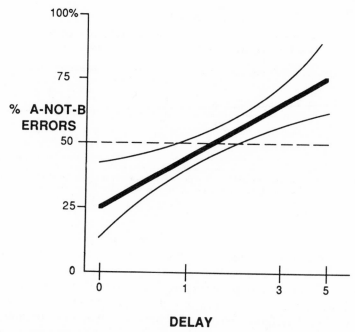

DELAY

FIG. 1.—Regression line and confidence bands for percentage of A-not-B errors. Delays are measured in seconds and are transformed as explained in the text to make the relation between delay and errors linear.

be expected by chance alone, and, conversely, at the longer delays, they are making more errors than would be expected by chance.

Table 3 summarizes the results for 8-, 9-, and 10-month-old infants.[5] A plus (+) in this table indicates that .50 was below the confidence band, a zero (0) indicates that .50 lies within the confidence band, and a minus (−) indicates that .50 was above the confidence band. (Thus, the pattern of pluses, zeros, and minuses for the 9-month-olds duplicates the information provided in Fig. 1.) Since a plus indicates more A-not-B errors than expected by chance, Table 3 shows that 8- and 9-month-old infants were perseverating at the longer delays. Since a minus indicates fewer A-not-B errors than expected by chance, Table 3 shows that 9- and 10-month-old

[5] The age values in Table 3 have a different meaning than those in Table 2. In Table 2 age is represented by a range of values for the purposes of tabulating studies. In Table 3, however, three specific values of age were chosen (8, 9, and 10 months), along with four values of delay (0, 1, 3, and 5 sec), for the purpose of constructing confidence intervals around the obtained regression plane. The goal of constructing confidence intervals at these 12 value combinations is to illustrate the effect of age and delay on infant errors relative to the random search model.

TABLE 3

COMPARISON OF THE OBTAINED REGRESSION LINE WITH THE LINE
PREDICTED BY THE RANDOM SEARCH MODEL: TWO-LOCATION
CONDITIONS ONLY

	DELAY (Sec)			
AGE (Months)	0	1	3	5
8	0	0(+)	+	+
9	−	0	+	+
10	−	−	0	0

NOTE.—A "+" indicates that more infants erred than would be expected by chance, a "0" indicates that the frequency of errors was consistent with a random model, and a "−" indicates that fewer infants erred than would be expected by chance. The value in parentheses stems from the bootstrap analyses.

infants were searching correctly at the shorter delays. These results show that the random search model is never tenable; at no age are there only zeros. Further, the data on 9-month-olds reveal a pattern of both above-chance and below-chance perseverative search. We will pay special attention to the data for 9-month-olds since our data base is especially dense for that age. As Table 2 indicates, most studies have used 9-month-olds, and for 9-month-olds there are no empty cells in the design matrix of variables.

Bootstrap analysis.—The basic idea of the bootstrap is to replace the theoretical normal distribution by the empirical distribution formed by the data (N observations) (Freedman & Peters, 1984). One then repeatedly samples with replacement (B samples of size N) from this empirical distribution, each time computing the coefficients of the regression model and storing the results. When the procedure is completed, there are B estimates of each parameter, each computed on a randomly selected set of observations. The mean of these B estimates is the bootstrap estimate of the parameter; the standard deviation of the B estimates is used to estimate the standard error of each parameter.

The results from our bootstrap analyses replicated the earlier findings in all respects. Thus, the bootstrap confidence intervals yielded nearly the same pattern of pluses, zeros, and minuses as appears in Table 3. The single exception is noted in parentheses in the table.

OMNIBUS TWO-LOCATION ANALYSES

Conditions were included in the previous analysis only if they met our somewhat stringent criteria for "standard" tasks. As a result, the number of conditions included was modest. Next, we conducted a similar analysis on a

TABLE 4

NUMBER OF CONDITIONS AND STUDY IDENTIFICATION NUMBERS
FOR THE OMNIBUS TWO-LOCATION ANALYSES

AGE (Months)	DELAY (Sec)				
	0	1–2	3	5–7	Total
8.0–8.9	0	2	8	4	14
9.0–9.9	5	5	20	2	32
10.0–11.9	1	0	8	0	9
Total	6	7	36	6	55
	NUMBER OF A TRIALS				
	1	2	3	4–8	Total
8.0–8.9	2	1	5	6	14
9.0–9.9	3	4	11	14	32
10.0–11.9	2	0	2	5	9
Total	7	5	18	25	55

NOTE.—Study identification numbers are 1a–b, 3a, 6a–b, 7a–b, 8a–f, 9a–f, 10a–f, 11d–f, 15a–d, 16a, 17a–c, 18a, 19a–e, 20a, 21a–b, 22a–b, 23a–b, 24a–c, 25a, 26a, and 29a.

larger array of conditions. We examined the effects of the same independent variables—age, A trials, delay, and year—using nonstandard conditions as well as the standard conditions used in the previous analyses. Twenty-four additional nonstandard conditions were included, yielding an omnibus data set with 55 data points. The nonstandard conditions included search tasks in which, for example, the orientation was vertical rather than horizontal (Butterworth, 1976), in which the hiding locations were displaced in either direction from the child's midline (Butterworth, 1975), in which curtains were used to control the sequence of hidings (Harris, 1973), or in which distractions were present during hiding (Frye, 1980). The essential criteria for inclusion in the omnibus data set were that only two identical locations were used and that the infant's error could be properly construed as an A-not-B error. Thus, the standard two-location analyses represent an admittedly strict and theoretically conservative approach to pooling data across studies, whereas the current analysis provides a complementary lenient approach yielding a more heterogeneous but more comprehensive sample of studies.

The frequency breakdown for the 55 conditions satisfying the essential criteria is shown in Table 4. Note that, even with this increased sample of studies, empty cells occur in the design for 8- and 10-month-olds. Thus, once again our findings for 9-month-olds will be of focal importance.

Regression analysis.—The same transformations used in the standard analysis were used in this analysis. The results of the stepwise regression of errors were essentially identical to those in the earlier analysis. Delay and age were the important factors in the regression, while A trials and year contributed little. The F ratios for delay and age, respectively, are $F(1,53) = 16.41$, $F(1,52) = 15.58$, p's $< .001$. The F ratios for A trials and year, respectively, are $F(1,51) = 1.45$, $F(1,50) < 1$. None of the two-variable interactions contributes beyond the main effects. In the cases of age $\times$ A trials and age $\times$ delay, F's < 1. In the case of A trials $\times$ delay, $F(1,50) = 2.01$, $p > .10$. If only delay and age are used in the linear model for errors, $R^2 = .41$, and the following coefficients are obtained:

$$\text{perseverative errors} = 8.9 - 1.5[\text{age}] + 2.3[\text{delay}]. \qquad (2a)$$
$$(1.2) \qquad (0.6) \qquad (0.5)$$

Comparing this model to that in (1a) shows the close comparability of the findings in the omnibus and standard two-location analyses.

Outlier analysis.—Three outliers were identifiable in a plot of the residuals against predicted values. These scores, in normalized form, are 2.56, -2.60, and -2.65, where 99% of such scores should be between 2.6 and -2.6. The t statistic for the positive residual (which has the smallest normal deviate form) is $t(51) = 4.15$, $p = .0005$.

One of the large negative residuals corresponds to condition 23b (Horobin & Acredolo, 1986) already discussed. The other negative residual corresponds to condition 6b, from Butterworth's study (1975, Experiment 1) of the effects of relative positioning on the A-not-B error. In that condition, the A location was at the infant's midline. Only 10% of the infants committed the error, far less than would otherwise be expected for 9-month-old infants at a delay of 3 sec. The condition of the large positive residual was 22a and came from Harris's (1973, Experiment 3) study of the effects of proactive interference. In this condition, a curtain was lowered at the A location after the object was hidden at the B location. Seven out of 10 infants made an A-not-B error, far more than would be expected from 10-month-olds with no delay.

Again, the outliers inflated the mean square error of the regression. If the outliers are omitted, R^2 increases from .41 to .60, but the coefficients remain substantially the same (cf. eq. [2a]):

$$\text{errors} = 8.2 - 1.5[\text{age}] + 3.0[\text{delay}]. \qquad (2b)$$
$$(1.0) \qquad (0.3) \qquad (0.5)$$

Confidence bands.—When confidence bands are constructed for the model in equation (2b), the resulting pattern of pluses, minuses, and zeros is identical to that found in Table 3.

TABLE 5

Number of Conditions and Study Identification Numbers
for the Standard Multilocation Analyses

Age (Months)	Delay (Sec)				
	0	1–2	3	5–15	Total
Two-location conditions:					
8.0–8.9	0	2	4	1	7
9.0–9.9	3	5	12	2	22
10.0–11.9	1	0	4	0	5
Total	4	7	20	3	34
Multilocation conditions:					
8.0–8.9	0	0	4	0	4
9.0–9.9	0	3	9	0	10
10.0–16.6	0	1	4	3	10
Total	0	4	17	3	24

Note.—Study identification numbers are 1a–b, 2a, 3a–b, 9a–f, 11d–f, 13a–c, 14a–d, 15a–c, 16a, 17a, 19a–e, 20a, 21a–b, 23a–c, 24a–c, 25a, 26a–b, 27a–b, 28a–h, 29a–b, and 30a–c.

STANDARD MULTILOCATION ANALYSES

So far our analyses have included two-location tasks. Several investigators (e.g., Cummings & Bjork, 1983a, 1983b; Sophian & Sage, 1985; and Sophian & Wellman, 1983) have used multilocation tasks to study infants' search for a hidden object. The provision of more than two locations makes it possible for the infant to err in a fashion other than returning to A. The occurrence of such nonperseverative errors has been taken as an index of children's memory for the hiding information. Intriguingly, infants are often reported to make fewer perseverative errors on multilocation tasks than on two-location tasks. For several reasons, therefore, it is important to include studies of multilocation tasks in the meta-analysis.

Including standard multilocation studies along with standard two-location conditions resulted in a total of 58 conditions, as shown in Table 5. Standard multilocation conditions met the criteria for standard two-location conditions but used more than two search locations. The addition of multilocation conditions required that two dependent variables be examined—perseverative errors and correct searching—since it was now possible for the infant to search at a location that was neither the initial location nor the correct location.

The addition of the multilocation conditions also requires an adjustment to the dependent variables since the expectation due to random searching differs according to the number of locations. In the two-location task the expected proportion of A-not-B errors according to the random search model was .50, but now the expected proportion varies from .50 (for two-location conditions) to .167 (for six-location conditions). In order to account for this variation, we used an adjusted proportion for each condition that was essentially a Z score. This Z score was obtained by subtracting the expected proportion (P) under the random search model from the observed proportion (p) and then dividing the difference by its standard deviation:

$$Z = \frac{p - P}{[p(1 - p)]^{1/2}}. \tag{3}$$

The theoretical rationale for this transformation derives from treating the observed proportion as a random variable with a binomial distribution (see Snedecor & Cochran, 1980). This same adjustment was appropriate for the proportions of both perseverative errors and correct searches.

We feel that this adjusted measure is needed to compare results across conditions correctly when the number of locations differs. However, it is also informative to inspect and analyze the unadjusted data—the proportions of infants erring and performing correctly in the various conditions. Those data and analyses of them are also provided.

Perseverative Errors

Regression analysis.—Bivariate plots of the dependent variable—perseverative errors as measured by the error Z score, termed "Z errors"—against each of the independent variables—age, A trials, delay, number of locations, and year—revealed a curvilinear relation between age and Z errors and between delay and Z errors. Consequently, delay was transformed using the transformation ln(delay + 1); for age we used the transformation ln(age − 7). Age was not transformed in the two-location analyses; however, in the multilocation analyses there was a greater range of ages (extending up to 16 months), and a curvilinear function was necessary to model this relation over the extended range.

Correlations between the six focal variables—year, age, A trials, delay, locations, and Z errors—indicated a significant ($p < .01$) relation between Z errors and age ($r = -.37$) and between Z errors and delay ($r = .34$). These correlations replicate the results of the two-location analyses. In addition, there was a significant correlation between Z errors and locations ($r = -.34$), indicating that having more locations decreased the likelihood of infants making a perseverative error. A trials correlated significantly with age ($r = -.34$), indicating that researchers have tended to use fewer A trials with older subjects over the increased age range available in this analysis. Finally, year of publication correlated significantly with number of A trials ($r = -.36$), replicating the finding in the two-location analyses that researchers have tended to use fewer A trials over the years. Year of publication also correlated significantly with locations ($r = .45$), indicating that researchers have tended to use more locations over the years.

The stepwise regression of Z errors on the five independent variables indicated that age, delay, and locations were the important influences in the regression, whereas A trials and year contributed little. The corresponding F ratios for the three significant variables are as follows: age, $F(1,56) = 8.71$; delay, $F(1,55) = 18.43$; and locations, $F(1,54) = 13.34$, p's $< .001$. The F ratios for A trials and year were both less than one. If A trials and year are dropped from the model, then $R^2 = .48$, and the following coefficients are obtained (with standard errors in parentheses):

$$Z \text{ errors} = 0.4 - 3.6[\text{age}] + 4.6[\text{delay}] - 1.4[\text{locations}]. \qquad (4a)$$
$$\phantom{Z \text{ errors} =} (1.4) \quad\quad (0.8) \quad\quad\quad (0.9) \quad\quad\quad (0.4)$$

Tests were made of the two-factor interactions. Only the age × locations interaction made a significant contribution to the model in (4a), $F(1,52) = 4.26$. For the age × delay and delay × locations interactions, $F < 1$. Although it was statistically significant, we decided not to include the age × locations interaction in the model since the gain in explanatory value—R^2 increases from .48 to .52—is small relative to the loss in parsimony. Furthermore, the age × locations interaction is highly correlated with other terms in the model (e.g., the correlation between age alone and the interaction is .91).

Outlier analysis.—One outlier was identifiable in the plot of the residuals against predicted values. This negative residual had a unit normal deviate value of -2.92, $t(53) = -3.40$, $p = .001$. The residual corresponds to condition 23b (Horobin & Acredolo, 1986). If the outlier is removed, then the coefficients for age, delay, and locations are virtually unchanged; however, R^2 increases from .48 to .54.

Confidence bands.—We constructed confidence bands around the linear model in (4a) to determine if these bands included the error values hypothesized by the random search model. The results are presented in Table 6. The entries in Table 6 have the same meaning as the entries in Table 3, with a single exception. In Table 3 the goal was to see if .50 was included in the confidence band since that was the value corresponding to the random search model for two-location tasks. The goal now is to see if zero is included within the regression bands since that is the value predicted by the random search model for the Z scores used in the multilocation analyses. As was the case in Table 3, in Table 6 the pluses indicate performance at above-chance

TABLE 6

Comparison of the Obtained Regression Line with the Line
Predicted by the Random Search Model: Perseverative
Errors in Multilocation Tasks

		DELAY (Sec)		
AGE (Months)	0	1	3	5
Two locations:				
8	0	0	+	+
9	−	0(−)	+	+
10	−	−	0	+(0)
Multilocations:				
8	0	0	+	+
9	−	−	0	+
10	−	−	0(−)	0

NOTE.—Values in parentheses stem from the bootstrap analyses.

levels, the minuses indicate performance below chance levels, and the zeros indicate performance that is consistent with a random hypothesis.

The portion of Table 6 corresponding to two-location tasks is identical to Table 3; thus, the original findings have not been distorted by including multilocation conditions. The lower portion of Table 6 indicates that, with more locations, infants are less often perseverative.

Bootstrap analysis.—As was the case with the standard two-location analysis, the bootstrap confidence intervals yielded nearly the same pattern of pluses, zeros, and minuses as before. There were only three minor discrepancies, noted in Table 6.

Unadjusted errors.—The preceding analyses show that Z errors decrease with increasing locations. Since this Z score compares errors to a chance baseline (.50 for two locations, .33 for three locations, etc.), two possibilities exist with respect to the absolute proportion of perseverative errors made. Absolute perseverative errors might decrease as number of locations increases, comparable to Z errors. However, they might stay constant (or even increase slightly) as well; if this were the case, the decrease in Z errors with increasing locations would reflect only the decreasing nature of the chance baseline as number of locations increases. It is thus important to inspect the unadjusted numbers of errors as well.

A regression analysis of the independent variables on errors yields the same substantive results as in the regression analysis of Z errors. In particular, number of locations remains a significant negative predictor of errors: locations, $F(1,56) = 48.87$, $p < .001$; age, $F(1,55) = 10.98$, $p < .001$; and delay, $F(1,54) = 23.73$, $p < .001$. A trials, $F(1,53) = 1.78$, and year, $F < 1$,

TABLE 7

PROPORTION OF PERSEVERATIVE ERRORS BOTH AS PREDICTED
BY THE REGRESSION MODEL AND AS OBSERVED
IN THE ORIGINAL STUDIES

A. PREDICTED

	DELAY (Sec)			
AGE (Months)	0	1	3	5
Two locations:				
8	.40	.56	.71	.77
9	.29	.44	.60	.68
10	.24	.37	.53	.63
Three locations:				
8	.34	.49	.65	.72
9	.25	.37	.53	.62
10	.20	.31	.46	.55

B. OBSERVED

	DELAY (Sec)			
AGE (Months)	0	1–2	3	5–15
Two locations:				
8.0–8.9	. . .	. . .	.70	. . .
9.0–9.9	.14	.49	.67	. . .
10.0–11.9	. . .	. . .	.32	. . .
Multilocations:				
8.0–8.9	. . .	. . .	.26	. . .
9.0–9.9	. . .	.36	.06	. . .
10.0–16.9	. . .	. . .	.09	.37

NOTE.—Observed results are averaged across all conditions in a cell; they are reported only where three or more conditions are available (see Table 5).

remain nonsignificant. If A trials and year are dropped from the model, then $R^2 = .69$, and the following coefficients are obtained:

$$\text{errors} = 10.79 - .24[\text{age}] + .26[\text{delay}] - 2.01[\text{locations}]. \qquad (4b)$$

Table 7 provides an analog version of Table 6. Rather than pluses and minuses comparing the regression plane to chance values, this table shows predicted values of the proportion of errors expected at different values of the independent variables based on the model in (4b). In addition, observed mean values are shown for any cells in the matrix in which the number of conditions available is three or more. As shown by the inclusion of locations as a significant predictor in the regression and by the predicted values in Table 7, the absolute likelihood of making a perseverative error decreases as the number of locations increases.

Correct Searching

Regression analysis.—As with perseverative errors, bivariate plots of the proportion correct Z score revealed curvilinear relations with age and delay. Hence, the same transformations used in the previous multilocation analyses were used in the analysis of correct searches.

Correlations between the six variables—year, age, A trials, delay, locations, and Z correct—indicated significant ($p < .01$) correlations between Z correct and age ($r = .42$) and between Z correct and locations ($r = .65$), which mirror the same correlations with perseverative errors. In this case, there was also a significant correlation between correct searches and year ($r = .42$), indicating that more correct searches have been reported in later publications. Of course, the correlations among the independent variables did not change from the analysis of errors since the data set and the transformations are identical to those used there.

The results of the stepwise regression of Z correct searches on the five independent variables showed that age, delay, and locations are the important carriers in the regression, with A trials and year contributing little: locations, $F(1,56) = 40.00$, $p < .001$; age, $F(1,55) = 12.77$, $p < .001$; delay, $F(1,54) = 35.43$, $p < .001$; A trials, $F < 1$; and year, $F(1,53) = 1.84$, $p > .20$. If A trials and year are dropped from the model, then $R^2 = .71$, and the following coefficients are obtained:

$$Z \text{ correct} = -4.8 + 4.8[\text{age}] - 5.5[\text{delay}] + 3.5[\text{locations}]. \quad (5a)$$
$$(1.5) \quad (0.8) \quad (0.9) \quad (0.4)$$

Further tests were made to determine if any of the two-factor interactions would make a contribution to the model in (5a). The F-to-enter values for all six two-factor interactions were nonsignificant ($p > .05$).

Outlier analysis.—One outlier was again identifiable (Horobin & Acredolo, 1986). It had a unit normal deviate value of 2.84, $t(53) = 3.31$, $p = .001$. With the outlier removed, equation (5a) is essentially unchanged, but R^2 increases from .71 to .75.

Confidence bands.—As before, we constructed confidence bands around the linear model in (5a) to determine if these bands included correct search values hypothesized by the random search model. The results of this analysis are presented in Table 8. The pluses in Table 8 indicate performance above chance levels, the minuses indicate performance below chance levels, and the zeros indicate performance that is consistent with a random hypothesis. Note, however, that the interpretation of the symbols in Table 8 is different than in Table 6 since performance here refers to correct, not perseverative, search. In Table 6 a plus indicates greater-than-chance perseveration, whereas in Table 8 a plus indicates greater-than-chance correct search.

TABLE 8

Comparison of the Obtained Regression Line with the Line
Predicted by the Random Search Model: Correct
Searches in Multilocation Tasks

	Delay (Sec)			
Age (Months)	0	1	3	5
Two locations:				
8	0	0	–	–
9	+	0(+)	–	–
10	+	+	0	–(0)
Multilocations:				
8	+	0	0	–
9	+	+	0(+)	0
10	+	+	+	0(+)

Note.—The values in parentheses stem from the bootstrap analyses.

Bootstrap analysis.—Again, bootstrap confidence intervals yielded nearly the same pattern of pluses, zeros, and minuses as before; the minor changes are noted in parentheses in Table 8.

Unadjusted correct searches.—For the same reasons that it was important to inspect the unadjusted proportions of errors made, it is also important to inspect the unadjusted proportion of correct searches. Once again, however, the data from Z correct and from the unadjusted proportions correct show the same trends. Most important, number of locations remains a significant positive predictor of correct searches. Delay, age, and locations are again significant carriers in the model, $F(1,56) = 11.14$, $p < .001$; $F(1,55) = 30.24$, $p < .001$; and $F(1,54) = 4.86$, $p < .05$, respectively; and year and A trials remain nonsignificant, F's < 1.

If the nonsignificant variables are dropped from the model, then $R^2 = .50$, and the following coefficients are obtained:

$$\text{correct searches} = 8.77 + .24[\text{age}] - .30[\text{delay}] + .47[\text{locations}]. \qquad (5b)$$

Table 9 provides an analog to Table 7, but with respect to correct searches.

DISTANCE AND DISTINCTIVENESS

In our analyses thus far, all locations and backgrounds within a condition have been identical (i.e., the locations were nondistinctive). However, researchers have at times varied the colors or other features of the covers or of the backgrounds of each location in order to make the locations visually distinctive. In addition, the distance between locations has varied across

TABLE 9

PROPORTION OF CORRECT SEARCHES BOTH AS PREDICTED BY THE
REGRESSION MODEL AND AS OBSERVED IN THE REPORTED STUDIES

A. PREDICTED

AGE (Months)	DELAY (Sec)			
	0	1	3	5
Two locations:				
8	.60	.41	.25	.19
9	.74	.58	.39	.30
10	.80	.67	.49	.38
Three locations:				
8	.75	.59	.40	.30
9	.83	.73	.57	.46
10	.88	.79	.66	.55

B. OBSERVED

AGE (Months)	DELAY (Sec)			
	0	1–2	3	5–15
Two locations:				
8.0–8.9	...	...	.30	...
9.0–9.9	.86	.51	.37	...
10.0–11.9	...	...	.68	...
Multilocations:				
8.0–8.9	...	...	.38	...
9.0–9.9	...	.46	.60	...
10.0–16.6	...	...	.84	.35

NOTE.—Observed results are averaged across all the conditions in a cell; they are
reported only where three or more conditions are available (see Table 5).

conditions and studies. Sufficient variation exists to test the influence of
these two additional factors, and these two factors provide evidence relevant
to several general accounts of infants' searching.

Our tests of distance and distinctiveness consider only two-location
studies. We included standard two-location search tasks (which used identical covers and backgrounds) for which information about the distance between locations was available (33 of the 34 conditions used in the standard
two-location analysis) and included as well corresponding two-location
search tasks in which the experimenter used either distinctive covers or
distinctive backgrounds ($N = 11$), for a total of 44 conditions (see Table 10).

Regression analysis.—Since age and delay have been shown to be important determiners of infant searching, they were included with distance and
distinctiveness in the regression analyses. As before, bivariate plots revealed
a curvilinear relation between errors and delay; hence, delay was transformed using the logarithmic transformation. In addition, errors were
transformed using the arcsine transformation.

TABLE 10

NUMBER OF CONDITIONS AND STUDY IDENTIFICATION NUMBERS
FOR THE DISTANCE AND DISTINCTIVENESS ANALYSES

Age (Months)	Nondistinctive	Distinctive	Total
8.0–8.9	7	3	10
9.0–9.9	21	5	26
10.0–11.9	5	3	8
Total	33	11	44

	DISTANCE (Cm) MEASURED CENTER TO CENTER				
	10–19	20–29	30–39	40–49	Total
8.0–8.9	0	1	6	3	10
9.0–9.9	4	3	6	13	26
10.0–11.9	1	0	6	1	8
Total	5	4	18	17	44

NOTE.—Study identification numbers are 1a–b, 3a, 4a, 5a, 9a–f, 11a–i, 12a–c, 15a–d, 16a, 17a, 19a–e, 20a, 21a–b, 23a–b, 24a–c, 25a, and 29a.

Distinctiveness was coded simply as 0 or 1 (0 = nondistinctive covers and backgrounds; 1 = distinctive covers or backgrounds). We conducted two analyses, each measuring distance in a different way. For the first, we defined distance between locations as the distance in centimeters between the centers of the two hiding locations. In the second, we used the distance in centimeters between the edges of the covers for the two locations. These two measures—center to center and edge to edge—are correlated, but by no means equivalent, $r(42) = .55, p < .01$. For example, condition 23b in Table 1 measured 46 cm center to center versus 41 cm edge to edge, whereas condition 19a measured 48 cm versus 18 cm. Most studies (9, 11, 12, 15, 16, 17, 19, 20, 21, 24, 25, and 29—see Table 1) reported how far apart the locations were in terms of an edge-to-edge distance. We converted this to a center-to-center measure by using reported information about the dimensions of the locations themselves.

Correlations between the six variables—age, delay, the two measures of distance, distinctiveness, and perseverative errors—yielded significant correlations between age and errors and between delay and errors, replicating our previous findings. In addition, there was a moderate correlation between distinctiveness and errors ($r = -.30, p < .05$), indicating that there are fewer errors when distinctive rather than nondistinctive locations are used. The correlations between distance, measured in either fashion, and errors were negligible ($r = -.15, .16$).

The results of the stepwise regressions indicated that age, delay, and distinctiveness were the important carriers in both of the regressions. Dis-

27

TABLE 11

Comparison of the Obtained Regression Line with the Line Predicted by the Random Search Model: Distance and Distinctiveness Analyses

	Delay (Sec)			
Age (Months)	0	1	3	5
Nondistinctive covers:				
8	0	0	+	+
9	−	0	+	+
10	−	−	0	0
Distinctive covers:				
8	0	0	0	0
9	−	−	0	0
10	−	−	−	0

tance measured in either fashion contributed little, F's < 1. When only age, delay, and distinctiveness were used in the linear model for errors, then $R^2 = .52$, and the following coefficients were obtained:

$$\text{perseverative errors} = 8.6 - 1.7[\text{age}] + 2.8[\text{delay}]$$
$$(1.3) \quad (0.4) \quad\quad (0.7)$$
$$- 1.8[\text{distinctiveness}].$$
$$(0.7)$$

(6)

Further tests revealed that none of the two-way interactions would make a contribution to the model in (6) (p's $> .05$).

Outlier analysis.—An analysis of residuals revealed a single outlier in the distance/distinctiveness data set. Its unit normal deviate value was -2.69, $t(39) = 3.06$, $p < .003$. The corresponding condition was 23b (Horobin & Acredolo, 1986). Only six out of 56 infants committed the A-not-B error in condition 23b, which is far less than would be expected given an average age of about 9 months and a delay of 3 sec. The distance involved in this condition was not abnormally wide given center-to-center measurements, 46 cm. For example, in Appel & Gratch (1984), Evans (1973), and Gratch et al. (1974), the distance between containers was about 48 cm, measured center to center. Given edge-to-edge measurements, however, Horobin and Acredolo's wide condition was wider (41 cm) than other conditions, which ranged from 7 to 36 cm. However, as shown above, even when measured in this fashion, distance had no influence on errors in the meta-analysis. In short, other two-location conditions of varying widths find substantially more perseverative errors than were found in condition 23b.

Confidence bands.—Table 11 presents the results from the analysis of confidence bands for the model in equation (6). The meaning of the symbols is the same as it was in Table 3: a plus indicates that .50 was below the confidence band, a zero indicates that .50 was within the confidence band, and a minus indicates that .50 was above the confidence band. The pattern of pluses, minuses, and zeros in the upper half of Table 11—corresponding to conditions with nondistinctive covers—is identical to the pattern shown in Table 3. The pattern of symbols in the lower half of the table—corresponding to conditions with distinctive covers—shows no perseveration at any age and correct searching at the shorter delays for the 9- and 10-month-old infants.

IV. DISCUSSION

Meta-analyses have both strengths and weaknesses. At best, they can be no better than the accumulated studies to date. They can, of course, be worse. Integrating information across studies in some manner is indispensable. A single study cannot be definitive; convergent findings are needed both to establish a phenomenon and to place it within a larger context of related findings and factors. The comparison, then, must be between some sort of quantitative integration of findings and more qualitative reviews. Purely qualitative reviews are more vulnerable to the biases of the reviewer and may reflect tendencies to ignore troublesome results unsuited to some prior theoretical commitment. In addition, it is often difficult simply to handle the numerous relevant studies (Green & Hall, 1984). Statistical methods protect against these problems by enabling the reviewer to integrate a large set of findings comprehensively and to uncover important effects pooled across studies that may not be apparent in a group of studies each with weak or conflicting findings.

Meta-analyses are subject to characteristic limitations. One concerns the pooling of studies of differing quality, the possibility of "garbage in—garbage out" (Eysenck, 1978, p. 517). We have taken several steps against such a possibility in our analyses. Our two-location analyses include both a strictly chosen subset of studies (the standard analysis) and a more inclusive sample as well (the omnibus analysis). The latter closely replicated the former. Another check involves entering year of publication into the analysis (Green & Hall, 1984). Often, a finding that appears intriguing in its first demonstrations shrinks or disappears as later experiments are devised with better controls. The growing number of recent reports of nonperseverative search in infants might have been due to such a trend. However, year of publication had no effect. As yet another check, we have taken care to look for outliers. The results cluster tightly with the exception of only a few outliers.

A second and related problem concerns nonreported findings, particularly the fact that findings of null results often remain unpublished. Our meta-analysis addresses this problem in several ways. First, we have sampled unpublished as well as published research extensively. Second, for many years investigators were unconcerned with whether perseverative errors exceeded some chance level of response. Any indication of search at A was interpreted as perseveration. Coupled with the exclusive use of two-location search tasks, this has insured that published studies include a wide range of levels of search at A. More recently, comparisons to chance have been routinely conducted. However, the recent literature is also replete with studies revealing both above-chance and below-chance levels of perseveration because the occurrence of perseveration itself has become a focal issue. This range of findings was in fact one of the original motivations for conducting a meta-analysis. Third, that the findings themselves are so logically and systematically organized—above-, at-, and below-chance findings arrange themselves in extremely orderly fashion (see Tables 3, 6, and 8) with respect to factors that have been nonsystematically explored by individual investigators—suggests that the findings are unlikely to be the artifact of either experimenter or publication biases.

A third issue for meta-analyses concerns how findings are quantified and pooled. In most cases, meta-analyses must pool indirect measures of effect significance (e.g., p values), and even these are not always reported precisely (e.g., $p < .05$). Much of the literature, and many of the controversies, surrounding meta-analysis involves this question of quantitative pooling of the findings and concerns the appropriateness, assumptions, and robustness of various techniques for this purpose. Our analyses avoid many of these issues. The measure being pooled is a direct one—proportions of children searching at a location—rather than a derived measure from a variety of different inferential statistical treatments in the different studies. Further, we have checked our analyses and analysis assumptions by computing our statistics with and without certain data transformations and, in addition, by using more assumption-free bootstrapping methods as well.

Throughout, the results were amazingly robust. Specifically, number of A trials was consistently unrelated to performance, whereas delay, subject age, and number of locations consistently had quite significant effects. Not only were these latter factors significant, but including them and them alone in several regression models allowed us to explain more than half the variance. Indeed, if one knows the length of delay, the number of locations, and the age of the subjects, then one can predict the errors and correct searches of a group of infants with an R^2 of approximately .50–.75. This is a strong accounting of the variances since in meta-analyses there are a host of factors that typically attenuate statistical accounts: in our case, differences across studies in experimenter characteristics and expertise, differences in the countries and child-rearing cultures sampled, and differences in the exact stimuli and procedures used.

The strengths of our analysis are coupled with some clear weaknesses. The most general limitation concerns the number of studies available and their distributions with respect to the relevant factors. Tables 2, 4, 5, and 10 reveal that the extant studies do not compose a clean experimental design, with all factors equally represented across the cells. However, the literature is sufficiently large and varied to be reasonably organized around the factors we have chosen. Deserving of particular mention is the distribution of studies with respect to age of subjects. Nine-month-olds are well studied, but younger and older infants have received much less attention. For this reason, we interpret the data as presenting a picture of, essentially, 9-month-old search. The main effect of age—that infants err less as they get older—seems clear and reliable, but any detailed analysis of changes in the pattern of infants' performance with increasing age seems untenable. In what follows, we emphasize the findings for 9-month-olds; this is where the strengths of our data lie.

Using these meta-analytic methods, a variety of substantive results emerge. We will discuss the results by comparing them to a range of predicted findings posited by the extant theories of stage 4 infant search. A general characterization of the results can be made at the outset that sets the stage for this elaborated discussion—namely, at every age, both above-chance and below-chance performance was observed. That is, at each age, and especially clearly for 9-month-olds, (a) at least one combination of delay and number of locations yielded above-chance A-not-B errors (see Table 6), and (b) some alternate combination of delay and number of locations yielded below-chance errors and significant above-chance correct performance (see Table 8). These conclusions hold across the slight variation in exact pattern of findings when our least-squares and bootstrap analyses are compared. These findings, appropriately elaborated, can be used to evaluate all extant theories of stage 4 infant search.

EVALUATION OF EXTANT THEORETICAL ACCOUNTS

Since Piaget's (1954) original formulation, several investigators have proposed theories to account for stage 4 search behavior. The theories themselves can be considered as ordered sets. Our organization mirrors the one outlined in Chapter I. We first consider "simple" theories, that is, those that clearly predict either random or above-chance perseverative or above-chance correct search for infants in the A-then-B search task. Next, we consider theories that predict a more complex pattern of both correct and perseverative search, which we term "combined components models." In this discussion, we will also address the sorts of processes posited by each theory to mediate the predicted behavior patterns. While all theories that predict a complex pattern of results posit multiple interactive processes to account for infants' behavior, this is also true for some theories that predict a simple pattern of results.

Simple Random, Perseverative, or Correct Search Models

The presence of above-, at-, and below-chance responding in various studies creates the suspicion that stage 4 search may simply be random. However, a random model is clearly inconsistent with the data. Tables 3, 6, and 8 contain more than zeros alone. Similarly, the findings quickly dispense with the simple perseverative search model and the simple correct search model. The relevant data here are the occurrences of a combination of pluses and minuses for infants of the same ages.

These simple accounts, as we have termed them, are not straw men. Piaget's (1954) account is essentially a perseverative model, predicting perseverative search. It is clear from the richness and variety of the examples he presents that Piaget considers perseverative search to be pervasive, that is, to occur with two or more locations, with a variety of delays, and for most stage 4 children. Additionally, Piaget's theoretical explanation, based as it is on the child's learning during A trials to recreate the object at A, must predict that B-trial search will be perseverative. Piaget therefore does not predict the substantial correct search observable in young stage 4 infants. A further difficulty for a Piagetian account is the consistent lack of a relation between search performance on B trials and prior amounts of experience at A.

Bremner (1982), like Piaget, argues that above-chance perseverative search characterizes infants' performance. Unlike Piaget, he argues that A-trial experiences inform the child about the functions of various places rather than about procedures for re-creating the object. The stage 4 infant understands the permanence of objects but is only just learning the function of various places. In particular, experience with the container at A informs the child of that container's use for concealment. "Infants assign this function to place A as a result of A trial experience, and rely on this knowledge to guide future search" (Bremner & Knowles, 1984, p. 312). Thus, to the extent that an infant's B-trial search is nonrandom (i.e., guided by relevant information), it should be perseverative—returning to location A because of its functional meaning of concealment. Given this explanatory system, Bremner has no basis for predicting significant correct search from infants of the same age—location B has not yet acquired any functional value for concealment. Since it does not predict high levels of correct search, the account does not square with the meta-analysis. Bremner's account also seems to predict that B-trial performance is tied to A trials and thus should vary as A-trial experience varies, a hypothesis refuted by the meta-analysis.

Cummings and Bjork (1983a, 1983b), on the other hand, propose what is essentially a memory model to account for stage 4 search. In their account, infants are assumed to base their search on memory for the correct locations. Hence, to the extent that they are not random (i.e., do not simply forget), they should be correct. In this account, putative perseverative errors are regarded as an artifact of using two-location tasks and thus should not significantly differ from chance. This account therefore does not predict the observed above-chance perseverative search that is indeed exhibited by stage 4 infants. It should be clear, conversely, that significant perseverative search means that children remember some information about the A hiding on the later B trials. Any memory model for stage 4 search must account for this memory as well.

Even the random model, which we have used as our null hypothesis in the meta-analysis, has no important theoretical proponent. In his earlier writings, Butterworth (1975, 1977) proposed that infant search on the A-then-B problem should be at chance levels for two-location problems—50% should be at A and 50% at B. Butterworth proposed that, to solve search problems, the infant must encode the hidden object's position with respect to some frame of reference. The stage 4 task "generates a conflict between two *equiprobable* frames of reference" (Butterworth, 1977, p. 399). The infant codes the object both with respect to a body-centered, response-derived (i.e., egocentric) code and with respect to a more objective code based on other objects in the visual field (an allocentric code). On A trials these two codes converge, but on B trials the response-derived egocentric code specifies A while the visually derived allocentric code specifies B. As a result, the infant responds to each location 50% of the time. Since Butterworth explicitly predicted a 50% response to A on two-location problems, the findings of substantial above-chance perseverative responding on two-location problems (Table 3) are at distinct odds with this position. In addition, similar patterns of equiprobable response to A and to B should be predicted even if more than two locations are provided. This account is thus also unable to predict the increasingly *correct* search performance that is obtained when the numbers of possible locations are increased.

With regard to these "simple" models, the occurrence of both significant errors and significant correct search from 9-month-old infants in the meta-analysis is an extremely informative finding. This observed pattern of performance strongly suggests that perseverative search is neither as prevalent a phenomenon as is often assumed (Harris, 1983; Piaget, 1954) nor the product of artifactual aspects of a unique testing situation (Cummings & Bjork, 1983a, 1983b). This pattern of results further suggests that infant search is unlikely to be the straightforward product of any single process or spatial conception.

Combined Components Models

Gratch's and Harris's accounts.—Gratch (Gratch et al., 1974) and Harris (1983) acknowledge that stage 4 infants are at times correct and at times perseverative, depending on the delay interval between hiding and finding on the B trials. Both authors propose that perseverative search, which occurs at longer delays, reflects the child's conceptual understanding of objects. Here, Gratch essentially endorses Piaget's interpretation, adding only a straightforward "motor memory" addendum to deal with correct responses at 0-sec delays. "When the infants were free to search during that time (0-sec. condition) the [motor] 'set' guided them into correct search. However, when they had to maintain the set for a longer period of time, they then assimilated the hiding of the toy into their scheme of finding the toy at A" (Gratch et al., 1974, p. 77).

Harris, however, most recently (Harris, 1983, 1987) proposed an alternate "identity" theory of infants' search errors. He suggests that the child's conceptual problem is not one of an absence of object permanence but is rather a conceptual confusion as to whether he or she has seen the same object in two different hiding places (A and B locations) or has seen two different, identical objects. The child's problem concerns the identity of the hidden object rather than its permanence. When the infant searches at A, he is in effect searching for the exact red ball previously hidden at A, not for the identical but different red ball hidden at B.

In contrast to the conceptual component obvious in infant's perseverative search, both writers conclude that correct search results from a lower-level immediate motor "orientation" of the infant. That is, when the object is hidden, the child might be leaning toward the object itself, for example, perhaps even incipiently reaching for it as it is hidden at B; in the absence of a delay he or she merely continues this act. In these two theories, therefore, above-chance correct search (or below-chance perseverative errors) should occur only for very short delays. It is on this point that they fail to account for the pattern of the data as revealed by the meta-analysis. As Tables 3 and 8 show, correct responses can occur at longer delays, especially if more than two locations are used. In fact, the same delays that lead to perseverative search on two-location problems—and that thus must be sufficient to induce a conceptual rather than a motor set approach to the task—fail to produce perseverative errors for same-age children if more hiding places are involved. Compare, for example, performance for 9-month-olds at 3-sec delays in the top and bottom portions of Tables 6 and 8. In sum, correct search is more prevalent than such motor memory accounts would predict, and it occurs with longer delays than would be predicted.

Diamond's account.—Diamond (1985) proposes that there is some period of delay between hiding and searching that causes perseveration in each stage 4 infant. Shorter delays than this lead to correct responding, while longer delays than this produce deteriorated or random responding. Two tendencies are proposed to lie behind this pattern. One is a perseverative tendency that Diamond regards essentially as habit strength; reinforced trials of reaching to A impart a tendency to search at A even on B trials. The second is a tendency to search at B on the basis of remembering that the object was indeed hidden there. Since this correct tendency is based on recall memory for the hiding location, it decreases as the amount of delay between hiding and finding increases. At short delays, then, the memory strength is sufficient, and the tendency to go to B correctly prevails. At somewhat longer delays, memory strength wanes, and the response tendency to go to A prevails; thus, the infant searches perseveratively. At even longer delays, performance deteriorates to random levels.

One clear finding from the meta-analysis seems to contradict Diamond's account—the absence of any effect of number of A trials. Like Piaget's and Bremner's theories, Diamond's account seems to predict that perseveration, as a habit-strength tendency, will covary with A trials. It does not. Diamond acknowledges that one or two A trials may be sufficient to establish the response of searching at A. But still she says that success at A strengthens the tendency to reach to A. Thus, lack of an A-trial effect seems detrimental, if not fatal, to her account. In addition, a weaker but still plausible implication of Diamond's proposal is that, with increasing delay, children's performance should move from correct to incorrect to chance responding (e.g., +, −, 0, in Table 3, 6, or 8). However, the data consistently depict a correct to chance level to incorrect trend.[6]

In Diamond's proposal, correct responding receives theoretical precedence—correct responding is based on memory for the correct location, whereas perseveration results from a lingering motor habit. In Gratch's and Harris's accounts (and Piaget's), perseveration receives theoretical precedence—perseverative errors reflect genuine conceptual confusions, and correct searches result from a brief motor orientation to B. The pattern of findings in the meta-analysis suggests that correct and incorrect responding might better receive equal theoretical weight.

Sophian and Wellman's account.—Sophian and Wellman (1983) proposed an information-processing account of infant search, which was elaborated

---

[6] Strictly speaking, because we employed linear models, these trends could have been of only two types: +, 0, −, or −, 0, +. However, since we employed transformations to linearize inherently curvilinear relations, at a more fundamental level the models are curvilinear, and it would have been possible to observe the +, −, 0, pattern predicted by Diamond. We never observed this U-shaped pattern of curvilinearity; rather we found only logarithmic patterns.

by Sophian (1984; Sophian & Yengo, 1985). In that account, the child facing the standard A-then-B search problem has two conflicting pieces of information to guide search for the object on B trials. One piece is current information—the information that, in the current trial, the object is hidden at B. The other piece is prior information—the information that, in the previous A trials, the object was hidden at A. The conflicting information specifies both A and B as locations at which to search for the missing object. Adults, of course, know that current information takes precedence over prior information in situations such as this. Infants, however, at times search at A during B trials. They may do so because they forget the current information and then search on the basis of prior information, or they may remember both pieces of information but incorrectly select prior information as the basis for search. In this account, both correct and perseverative search are conceptually important—in both cases the children's search reflects attempts to guide search on the basis of potentially useful information. The problem made evident by perseverative errors is that infants may rely on inappropriate information.

First, we consider whether an explanation based simply on the forgetting of B information and hence the default utilization of A information can account for the findings. Such an explanation can easily predict the observed increase in perseverative search given increased delay between hiding and finding on B trials since, as the delay increases on the B trial, B information wanes. For such a model to predict significant perseveration (rather than just increases in perseveration), however, A information (which can also decay) must somehow be especially memorable. Several different memory accounts of this sort are possible: the A information may be especially memorable because of overlearning, primacy, or proactive interference. However, memory accounts of these sorts are difficult to square with the current findings on number of locations. An essential finding of the meta-analysis is the increasingly *correct* performance with increasing numbers of locations to search. Yet, in most memory accounts, increasing the number of (identical) locations can be expected to increase the infants' memory burden by increasing the difficulty of discriminating or remembering the single correct location from the pool of possible locations. This sort of expectation is obvious in Cummings and Bjork's (1983a, 1983b) discussion; it explicitly motivated Sophian and Wellman's (1983; Sophian, 1985) explanation for why they observed lower rates of perseveration with a three-location task than were observed in studies using two-location tasks; and memory performance certainly decreases when the number of identical locations is increased with preschool children (e.g., Wellman, Ritter, & Flavell, 1975).

Given this expectation, both perseverative performance and correct performance should decrease with increasing locations since both rest directly on memory for a single location within an array of possibilities. Perseverative errors do decrease, but, in addition, correct performance increases to significantly above chance levels. This finding points to the existence of some mediating factor other than memorability/confusability of the locations.

Of course, the mechanism that results in infants' searching on the basis of A information rather than B may be, not a memory-strength mechanism, but a choice mechanism. This is Sophian and Wellman's selectivity notion. Even when both A information and B information are remembered on B trials, the infant incorrectly bases search on A information. However, selectivity as proposed by Sophian and Wellman also does not easily conform to the present findings concerning the number of locations. The selectivity notion suggests that significant nonrandom performance results from selecting one form of information over another. Suppose 9-month-olds tend correctly to select current information as a basis for search. Then this selection of current information over prior fails to predict significant perseveration, which is also clearly observable. Similarly, if the model is adjusted to conclude that 9-month-old infants tend incorrectly to select prior over current information, then, while it successfully predicts above-chance perseverative search, it fails simultaneously to predict above-chance correct search. In short, consistent adoption of one sort of selection rule or the other does not account for the mixed results. What is needed from the point of view of this account is some factor tied to the number of locations that shifts the child's selection. Neither Sophian nor Wellman has ever proposed a way in which the number of locations influences selectivity (the original Sophian and Wellman proposal, as discussed above, had it affecting memory difficulty), and it is difficult to see how this would work. In short, Sophian and Wellman's account seems incompatible with or problematically silent on a major finding of the meta-analysis—the role of number of locations.

Horobin and Acredolo's account.—To reiterate, the meta-analysis reveals that increasing the number of locations increases correct performance (rather than merely lowering perseverative responding) and increases it to above-chance levels. This works against any memory explanation for the number-of-locations effect that is based on lack of discriminability between the containers. What, then, could account for this effect? The opposite possibility is that increasing the number of locations somehow increases rather than decreases the discriminability of the single correct location, thus enhancing correct performance. Horobin and Acredolo (1986) hypothesize that, since increasing the number of locations tends to increase the amount of distance between the end locations in the series, and since the A and B locations are often (though not always—see Cummings & Bjork, 1983a, 1983b) at opposite ends of the array, the difference between the A and B locations is clearer and more salient when more locations are used. Wide separations of A and B thus make it easier for an infant to discriminate and attend to the correct location.

The hypothesis that the number of locations functions by increasing the discriminability between A and B locations (via increasing their spatial separation) can be tested by comparing two-location problems with wide versus narrow distances between containers. Horobin and Acredolo did this, and their wide-pair condition yielded very few perseverative errors. However, in our meta-analysis of the effects of distance on two-location tasks, increasing distance had no influence on subjects' errors.

There are two reasons to consider our meta-analytic findings as strong refutation of the hypothesis that the number-of-locations effect is essentially a discriminability or attention effect that is due to distance. First, we conducted the analysis with two alternate measures of distance. In neither analysis was distance between locations a significant factor in accounting for children's errors. Moreover, at least with one measure of distance, several other studies also used quite wide separations between locations. Among these studies, the Horobin and Acredolo wide-pair results (condition 23b) were an outlier; other extant conditions using wide distances report higher levels of perseverative search. Second, and perhaps more telling, is that the discriminability argument, like the memorability argument discussed earlier, is based on assuming that children's search at A during B trials is due to confusion about which location is the proper B location. Infants essentially attempt to search at B and merely confuse A with B. On this account, search at A should never exceed chance levels (50% in two location problems) during B trials, the level expected in the case of complete confusability between A and B. As is clear from the meta-analysis, above-chance perseverative responding regularly occurs on tasks such as this. Infants search at A significantly more often than expected by chance alone (more than 50% in two-location studies) under several predictable circumstances, as is obvious in Tables 3 and 6.

Note that, in the analysis of distances, distinctiveness, as indexed by the presence or absence of distinctive covers or backgrounds, was shown to be a significant factor. Several studies have proposed that increased distinctiveness should increase correct search. However, individual tests of this hypothesis have yielded mixed results (e.g., Butterworth, Jarrett, & Hicks, 1982). When these results are pooled across studies, however, infants are clearly increasingly correct and decreasingly perseverative if the locations are made more distinctive. We emphasize again, however, that the data with respect to distinctiveness do not support a simple discriminability account of stage 4 errors. If errors to A were only the result of confusion about whether the object was hidden at A or B—a confusion reduced by using distinctive locations—then errors to A would never significantly exceed chance.

Butterworth's account.—Earlier, we outlined Butterworth's prediction of equiprobable search at A and B. In his more recent work (Butterworth & Jarrett, 1982; Butterworth et al., 1982), Butterworth proposes that equiprobable search is only to be expected given identical containers and locations. However, if the backgrounds differ (Butterworth & Jarrett, 1982), or if the locations differ against a stable background (Butterworth et al., 1982), then infants search more consistently. Recall that, in Butterworth's (1975, 1977) original account, equiprobable search results from a conflict between an egocentric and an allocentric method or code for discriminating A from B. In essence, he now argues that, given the proper "spatial characteristics of the environment," the infant can perceive that a single object has been relocated from one to another spatially discriminable hiding place. Thus, "successive locations on the same surface are discriminable . . . ; object localization does not *require* reference to an egocentric code to differentiate A from B" (Butterworth et al., 1982, p. 447). In short, egocentric conflicts can be circumvented provided that the spatial structure for the task is properly distinctive. But "where the background is continuous and the covers identical . . . the spatial structure of the task necessitates dependence on an egocentric code[, which gives] rise to a conflict between the self-referent code and the background, leading to the equiprobable pattern of search" (Butterworth et al., 1982, p. 447).

This account thus continues to predict equiprobable search when containers and backgrounds are identical. In our standard two-location and standard multilocation analyses, containers and backgrounds were identical. Butterworth's account predicts neither the above-chance errors nor the above-chance correct search clearly apparent in such circumstances (Tables 3, 6, and 8).

Summary.—This review shows that investigators have often proposed theories that account for the data of their own specific studies but that tend to ignore other available evidence; consequently, current theories are all inconsistent with the results of the meta-analysis in varying fashions and degrees. Thus, despite the plethora of current accounts, there is need for one more.

PROPOSED ALTERNATE ACCOUNT

In this section we propose a new account of infant object search, one consistent with the entire set of findings of our meta-analysis. This consistency is achieved post hoc; the account was designed to square with the obtained findings. Nonetheless, that this account is consistent with the obtained findings where others are not suggests its potential.

First, we posit that search for hidden objects can take place in two slightly different ways. Neither of these ways is proposed as an unthinking or nonconceptual approach to the problem—that is, neither is like Diamond's manual habit or like Harris's and Gratch's motor set. Both these ways, we propose, are approaches based on considerations of relevant information about the object's position in space. Nonetheless, one approach is more cognitively effortful, integrating more information over various times and locations, than the other. The first, more simple approach we term the "direct-finding approach." This encompasses the simplest possible solution to a search problem—searching directly where the object vanished. For example, you watch an object being hidden in a closet and to retrieve it simply go there; or you watch your keys as they drop into a wastebasket and to get them simply look there. Adults, children, and even infants often simply look for the object where it vanished from sight.

However, other search problems provoke, at least in adults and older children, a more integrative, inferential approach. For example, when you are looking for your lost dog, you attempt to figure out the animal's route and intercept him. Or you wish to retrieve a ball that rolled under the front of the couch; to do so, you go around to the rear to see if it rolled out the back side. In these cases, the searcher first imagines and/or infers a probable unwitnessed location for the object and searches there. These sorts of approaches we term "inferred-location approaches." An essential characteristic of objects is that they can be displaced in space over time; thus, we typically have access to only a small sample of their spatiotemporal path (Quinton, 1973). A corresponding characteristic of missing objects that thus requires some sort of inferred-location approach for optimal search performance is that they may be displaced after they disappear from view. The examples above vary considerably in the sorts of information integration needed to solve the search problem correctly. Still, they share two important features: (a) a direct-finding approach (i.e., searching directly where the object vanished) is likely to be incorrect, and (b) some sort of consideration of the object's displacement over time and space is required.

It is possible, of course, that for adults there is really only one sort of search approach, one that considers an object's current position as part of a spatiotemporal sequence of positions, even when an object is seen to be (directly) placed in a single container. For infants, however, there may well be differences in the cognitive effort and abilities required to conceive of the object's position in the simplest witnessed-disappearance case and in more and more complex moving-object cases. Specifically, whereas in the direct-finding approach the infant simply searches where the object was last seen, in the inferred-location approach the infant considers more information about the object—such as where it has been seen at other times—and conceives of a location on the basis of this enlarged data base.

How do these two approaches interact to determine stage 4 search?

41

Using a direct-finding approach, the infant simply considers where the object just vanished. Using an inferred-location approach, he or she attempts to infer the object's probable current location from its movements over locations and times. The A-then-B search task confronts the stage 4 infant with a problematic situation. Not only does the A-then-B problem itself have features that make it amenable to both sorts of search approaches, but the 9-month-old has cognitive capabilities that could also support both types of approach. The approach adopted directly determines errors; the approach adopted is jointly influenced by several different factors.

On the one hand, we propose, correct search on the A-then-B problem results from a direct-finding approach. The object is placed at B, and the infant searches for it directly at B. On the other hand, perseverative errors result from an inferred-location approach. That is, in certain simple circumstances, the infant approaches the problem with the goal of inferring the object's hidden location from its movements. That is, early in stage 4 we witness the first appearance of any sort of inferred-location approach to search problems. The inference involved is not formal, logical, or conscious; it simply integrates information about the object's spatiotemporal history into the decision-making process. This first utilization of the inferred-location approach is, however, a mixed blessing. That the infant adopts such an approach at all is a step toward the mature solution of a wide range of search problems—problems concerning invisibly displaced objects. However, adopting this more advanced approach, at first, means arriving at an erroneous (perseverative) solution.

The A-then-B problem presents the infant with information about the object's displacement over time and space; first it is at A, and then it is moved to B. Thus, there is information available about both prior and present locations. However, in the process of entertaining information about the object's prior location as relevant to conceiving of its current location at all, the classic stage 4 infant overvalues that information. At this point he or she tends to infer the object's location incorrectly on the basis of prior location information. Of course, in simple stage 4 search problems, prior location information is actually superseded by the current location information. Thus, for 9-month-olds the A-then-B problem is particularly provocative and problematic. The movement of the object from A to B is simple and clear and thus potentially within the infant's limited grasp. But the object's prior location at A is essentially irrelevant to its current location at B.

On this account, perseverative stage 4 errors are not the last vestige of the still younger infant's deficient conception of objects' permanent existence; stage 4 infants understand the permanence of objects. Perseverative errors are instead the first appearance of the infant's struggle correctly to infer an object's hidden location from information about its spatiotemporal movements. Such errors are growth errors. That still older infants have considerable difficulties dealing with object movements is indicated by their performances on visible and invisible displacement tasks and transposition tasks (Fisher & Jennings, 1981; Haake & Somerville, 1985; Piaget, 1954; Sophian & Sage, 1983).

The essence of our claim is that, given a nascent inferred-location approach, the stage 4 infant at times sees the A-then-B task in an inferred-location fashion, as if the task were to integrate object movement information (from prior trials to current ones) rather than to ignore it. When will the infant adopt this approach? At this early age, infants' laudable but mistaken attempts to deal with the stage 4 A-then-B task in a more advanced (inferred-location) manner are quite tenuous. Their initial impulse is a direct-finding one. Thus, (1) in many circumstances it occurs to the infant to utilize a (faulty) inferred-location approach only if his or her direct-finding impulse is initially inhibited. Most obviously, this may happen if there is a delay between hiding and finding. When a delay is imposed, the infant is not allowed to search for the object immediately. This provides an imposed opportunity to reflect rather than to search directly and thus influences whether the child adopts a direct-finding or a inferred-location approach (and this influences errors). For this reason perseveration is not observed at 0-sec delays between hiding and finding but appears and increases as delay increases. Similarly, if containers are identical rather than distinctive, the confusability between containers can inhibit an immediate direct-finding response and provoke a more reflective, inferred-location approach to the problem. Thus, perseveration increases as distinctiveness decreases.

On the other hand, (2) if the problem is altered so that an inferred-location approach is not engaged at all, then direct finding prevails. This happens when the number of locations is increased. In these cases, the many locations do not map easily and directly onto a single prior and a single current location. This makes it more difficult for the infant to conceive of the B-trial hiding as an extension in time and space of A-trial occurrences, and the problem is unlikely to facilitate an early, tenuous inferred-location approach. Lacking a facilitative problem, the infant never attempts to integrate A and B information together; he simply correctly searches at B via direct finding.

A potentially problematic part of our proposal is the attribution of an inferential approach to 9-month-old infants. Perseverative errors, by our account, stem from beginning use of an inferred-location approach, however tenuous and incorrect. We wish to reiterate, therefore, that we do not intend to credit the infant with conscious, deductive, inferential powers. We posit only a nascent tendency to attempt to integrate several frames of information from the object's spatiotemporal history to arrive at a pragmatic conception of the object's hidden location. We may be overstating the infant's capability by labeling this process an inference, even an inaccurate, pragmatic one. However, we have chosen this term to emphasize the continuity, as we see it, between the 9-month-old's nascent, inaccurate inferences in simple A-then-B tasks and the slightly older infant's accurate spatiotemporal inferences in even more complex tasks. For example, Haake and Somerville (1985) have shown that 15-month-olds can infer a hidden object's location correctly from a sequence of rather complex spatiotemporal information. Specifically, in a task involving the invisible displacement of objects, they can infer which of the visited locations contains the object on the basis of two pieces of information: (a) the last place the object was seen and (b) the first place it was known to be missing. It is plausible, therefore, that 9-month-olds may be beginning to wrestle with the spatiotemporal information eventually needed to support such later-developing correct inferences, that their attempts to do so are flawed, and that such flawed attempts account for perseverative search.

This newly proposed account is consistent with the comprehensive findings of the meta-analysis, but the meta-analysis does not provide a predictive test of the account. Still, two other sorts of data outside the scope of the meta-analysis lend credence to the account.

Search on A trials.—The proposed account affords an explanation of another important but often overlooked aspect of children's search behavior—their almost errorless performance on A trials, even on their first A trial. What if, as Piaget proposes, the infant believes that a hidden object is destroyed and then re-created by his own actions when found? Similarly, what if the infant believes that there are multiple identical objects available (Harris, 1983)? In either event, why should the infant search at A initially and not B? The B location is also a possible source of activity or of objects, and on this very first A trial the infant has no previous experience of recovering the object at A (and hence creating it by his actions). Admittedly, the child's attention has been drawn to A by the object hiding. But in these situations, infants are typically quite interested in all the available manipulable stimuli. Moreover, on B trials children's attention is drawn to B; yet they search at A anyway.

Throughout the studies of infant search, almost errorless A-trial performance is commonplace, though performance on first A trials is seldom discussed. A meta-analytic pooling of the findings is helpful here. Over all the studies in the meta-analysis, 19 provided information about first A-trial performance separated from performance for all A trials combined. The data represent 63 conditions involving only 8-, 9-, or 10-month-olds. Over these conditions, first A-trial performance averages 88% correct. This extremely high level of correct performance is difficult to explain without assuming that initially the infant searches at A because he believes a single object to be there and nowhere else, in advance of any direct manipulative experience with any of the containers. Hence, the present proposal has the advantage of assuming that A-trial search is straightforwardly explained by the fact that the infant searches at A via direct finding; he saw the object vanish there and searches for it directly where it vanished.

Object knowledge.—An important claim of this account (and several other recent explanations) is that stage 4 infants know about objects' permanence. Such an account would be strengthened by independent evidence that infants appreciate that hidden objects continue to exist. Recently, Baillargeon (in press; Baillargeon, Spelke, & Wasserman, 1985) has demonstrated an appreciation of object permanence in 5-, 6-, and 8-month-old infants. Infants were first habituated to a rectangular screen, hinged at its base, that moved back and forth through a 180-degree arc from flat and forward to upright to flat and backward (Baillargeon et al., 1985). After habituation, a box was positioned behind the screen, and infants were shown two test events, one a possible event and one an anomalous event. In the former, the screen swung from front to back, stopped appropriately when it touched the hidden box, and then swung forward again. In the anomalous case, it swung through the complete 180 degrees as if the hidden box were not there. Infants looked significantly longer at the anomalous event than at the possible event. This suggests that infants believed that the hidden box continued to exist and were puzzled when the screen did not stop on expected contact with the box. A control condition (in which the two test events involved the box sitting to the side of the screen rather than behind it) showed that the results were not due just to some preference for the one test event over the other; the results were specific to the case involving the hidden object. A further study with 6- and 8-month-olds (Baillargeon, in press) involving quite different test events led to similar results.

A classic difficulty for developmental psychology concerns reconciling the differences between different tasks purporting to measure the same construct. Thus, it is not immediately clear whether Piagetian object search tasks and Baillargeon's visual preference tasks capture object permanence in the same sense or what it means for 5- and 6-month-olds to pass Baillargeon's task and still fail to search for hidden objects. However, the meta-analysis shows that data from both tasks are convergent for 8- and 9-month-olds. In total, such stage 4 infants find visually displayed impermanence to be anomalous, search correctly for objects on A trials of A-then-B tasks, and can search for objects correctly on B trials as well (see Tables 3 and 9). In short, Baillargeon's findings significantly strengthen the claim that, by 8 and 9 months of age, infants understand the permanent existence of objects hidden from view. This in turn strengthens the plausibility of our proposal that the problem underlying the A-not-B error must be that of dealing with object movements, not object permanence.

V. CONCLUSIONS

The current meta-analysis organizes the available findings on stage 4 search, provides results contradictory to all extant accounts of stage 4 search, and inspires a new proposed account that motivates further research. Organizing the literature is a sizable accomplishment in itself since the current wealth of findings has seemed contradictory in the past. It is now clear that results are more orderly, consistent, and therefore informative than was previously apparent.

Once the findings are organized as in the meta-analysis, the merits and demerits of current competing accounts of early search become clear. This too is an important accomplishment because it points to a variety of mismatches between data and theory. Finally, the meta-analysis has resulted in the proposal of an empirically consistent account of stage 4 search. Such a proposal is, at the least, an important interim step to further research and theorizing.

The findings of the meta-analysis suggest several sorts of needed research. As one example, the concentration on 9-month-olds in the current literature means that our understanding of developments in search and conception in this volatile age range from 8 to 12 months is severely limited. As another, that infants' performance changes from significantly above chance perseveration to significantly above chance correct search as the number of locations is increased is a powerful, even puzzling, effect. With the exception of Horobin and Acredolo (1986), no studies have specifically investigated this effect.

The domain of infant search has been an especially lively one for investigation and an especially fertile one for development of theoretical accounts of infant cognition (Harris, 1983; Wellman, 1985). How to integrate the wealth of findings and how to evaluate the competing theories has been less clear. The meta-analysis integrates findings and provides a crucial testing ground for theory-building endeavors.

REFERENCES

Acredolo, L. P. (1978). Development of spatial orientation in infancy. *Developmental Psychology,* **14,** 224–234.

Acredolo, L. P., & Evans, D. (1980). Developmental changes in the effects of landmarks on infant spatial behavior. *Developmental Psychology,* **16,** 312–318.

Appel, K. J. (1971). *Three studies in object conceptualization: Piaget's sensori-motor stages four and five.* Unpublished doctoral dissertation, University of Houston.

Appel, K. J., & Gratch, G. (1984). Will infants search when "no toy" is hidden? A study of implicit assumptions about the development of object permanence. *British Journal of Developmental Psychology,* **2,** 179–188.

Baillargeon, R. (in press). Representing the existence and the location of hidden objects: Object permanence in six- and eight-month-old infants. *Cognition.*

Baillargeon, R., Spelke, E. S., & Wasserman, S. (1985). Object permanence in five-month-olds. *Cognition,* **20,** 191–208.

Bell, S. M. (1970). The development of the concept of the object as related to infant-mother attachment. *Child Development,* **41,** 291–311.

Bjork, E. L., & Cummings, E. M. (1984). Infant search errors: Stage of concept development or stage of memory development. *Memory and Cognition,* **12**(1), 1–19.

Bower, T. G. R., & Patterson, J. G. (1972). Stages in the development of the object concept. *Cognition,* **1,** 47–55.

Bremner, J. G. (1978). Spatial errors made by infants: Inadequate spatial cues or evidence of egocentrism? *British Journal of Psychology,* **69,** 77–84.

Bremner, J. G. (1982). Object localization in infancy. In M. Potegal (Ed.), *Spatial abilities: Developmental and physiological foundations* (pp. 76–106). New York: Academic Press.

Bremner, J. G. (1985). Object tracking and search in infancy: A review of data and a theoretical evaluation. *Developmental Review,* **5**(4), 371–396.

Bremner, J. G., & Bryant, P. E. (1977). Place versus response as the basis of spatial errors made by young infants. *Journal of Experimental Child Psychology,* **23,** 162–171.

Bremner, J. G., & Knowles, L. S. (1984). Piagetian stage IV search errors with an object that is directly accessible both visually and manually. *Perception,* **13,** 307–314.

Butterworth, G. (1975). Object identity in infancy: The interaction of spatial location codes in determining search errors. *Child Development,* **46,** 866–870.

Butterworth, G. (1976). Asymmetrical search errors in infancy. *Child Development,* **47,** 864–867.

Butterworth, G. E. (1977). Object disappearance and error in Piaget's stage IV task. *Journal of Experimental Child Psychology,* **23,** 391–401.

Butterworth, G., & Jarrett, N. (1982). Piaget's stage 4 error: Background to the problem. *British Journal of Psychology,* **73**(2), 175–185.

Butterworth, G. E., Jarrett, N., & Hicks, L. (1982). Spatio-temporal identity in infancy: Perceptual competence or conceptual deficit? *Developmental Psychology*, **18**(3), 435–449.

Cornell, E. (1978). Learning to find things: A reinterpretation of object permanence studies. In L. S. Siegel & C. J. Brainerd (Eds.), *Alternatives to Piaget: Critical essays on the theory* (pp. 1–27). New York: Academic Press.

Corter, C. M., Zucker, K. J., & Galligan, R. F. (1980). Patterns in the infant's search for mother during brief separation. *Developmental Psychology*, **16**, 62–69.

Cummings, E. M., & Bjork, E. L. (1983a). Perseveration and search on a five-choice visible displacement hiding task. *Journal of Genetic Psychology*, **142**, 283–291.

Cummings, E. M., & Bjork, E. L. (1983b). Search behavior on multi-choice hiding tasks: Evidence for an objective conception of space in infancy. *International Journal of Behavioral Development*, **6**, 71–87.

Diamond, A. (1985). Development of the ability to use recall to guide action, as indicated by infants' performance on $A\overline{B}$. *Child Development*, **56**, 868–883.

Draper, N. R., & Smith, H. (1981). *Applied regression analysis* (2d ed.). New York: Wiley.

Dunst, C. J., Brooks, P. H., & Doxsey, P. A. (1982). Characteristics of hiding places and the transition of stage IV performance in object permanence tasks. *Developmental Psychology*, **18**(5), 671–681.

Efron, B. (1982). *The jackknife, the bootstrap, and other resampling plans*. Philadelphia: Society for Industrial and Applied Mathematics.

Efron, B., & Gong, G. (1983). A leisurely look at the bootstrap, the jackknife, and cross-validation. *American Statistician*, **37**, 36–48.

Evans, W. F. (1973). *The stage IV error in Piaget's theory of object concept development: An investigation of the role of activity*. Unpublished dissertation proposal, University of Houston.

Evans, W. F., & Gratch, G. (1972). The stage IV error in Piaget's theory of object concept development: Difficulties in object conceptualization or spatial location? *Child Development*, **43**, 682–688.

Eysenck, H. J. (1978). An exercise in mega-silliness. *American Psychologist*, **33**, 517.

Fisher, K., & Jennings, S. (1981). The emergence of representation in search. *Developmental Review*, **1**, 18–30.

Freedman, D. A., & Peters, S. C. (1984). Bootstrapping a regression equation: Some empirical results. *Journal of the American Statistical Association*, **79**, 97–106.

Frye, D. (1980). Stages of development: The stage IV error. *Infant Behavior and Development*, **3**, 115–126.

Glass, G. V., McGaw, B., & Smith, M. L. (1981). *Meta-analysis in social research*. Beverly Hills, CA: Sage.

Gratch, G. (1972). A study of the relative dominance of vision and touch in six-month-olds. *Child Development*, **43**, 615–623.

Gratch, G. (1975). Recent studies based on Piaget's view of object concept development. In L. B. Cohen & P. Salapatek (Eds.), *Infant perception from sensation to cognition* (Vol. **2**, pp. 51–99). London: Academic Press.

Gratch, G., Appel, K. J., Evans, W. F., LeCompte, G. K., & Wright, N. A. (1974). Piaget's stage IV object concept error: Evidence of forgetting or object conception. *Child Development*, **45**, 71–77.

Gratch, G., & Landers, W. F. (1971). Stage IV of Piaget's theory of infants' object concepts: A longitudinal study. *Child Development*, **42**, 359–372.

Green, B. F., & Hall, J. A. (1984). Quantitative methods for literature reviews. *Annual Review of Psychology*, **35**, 37–53.

Haake, R. J., & Somerville, S. C. (1985). Development of logical search in infancy. *Developmental Psychology*, **21**, 176–186.

Harris, P. L. (1971). Examination and search in infants. *British Journal of Psychology*, **62**, 469–473.

Harris, P. L. (1973). Perseverative errors in search by young infants. *Child Development*, **44**, 28–33.

Harris, P. L. (1974). Perseverative search at a visibly empty place by young infants. *Journal of Experimental Child Psychology*, **18**, 535–542.

Harris, P. L. (1983). Infant cognition. In M. M. Haith & J. J. Campos (Eds.), P. H. Mussen (Series Ed.), *Handbook of child psychology: Vol. 2. Infancy and developmental psychobiology* (pp. 689–782). New York: Wiley.

Harris, P. L. (1987). The development of search. In P. Salapatek & L. B. Cohen (Eds.), *Handbook of infant perception* (Vol. 2). New York: Academic Press.

Horobin, K. M., & Acredolo, L. P. (1986). The role of attentiveness, mobility history, and separation of hiding sites on stage IV search behavior. *Journal of Experimental Child Psychology*, **41**, 114–127.

Jackson, E., Campos, C. C., & Fischer, K. W. (1978). The question of decalage between object permanence and person permanence. *Developmental Psychology*, **14**, 1–10.

Kramer, J., Hill, K., & Cohen, L. B. (1975). Infant's development of object permanence: A refined methodology and new evidence of Piaget's hypothesized ordinality. *Child Development*, **46**, 149–155.

Landers, W. F. (1968). *The effects of different amounts and types of experience on infants' object concepts.* Unpublished doctoral dissertation, University of Houston.

Landers, W. F. (1971). Effects of differential experience on infants' performance in a Piagetian stage IV object-concept task. *Developmental Psychology*, **5**, 48–54.

LeCompte, G. K., & Gratch, G. (1972). Violation of a rule as a method of diagnosing infants' level of object concept. *Child Development*, **43**, 385–396.

Meicler, M., & Gratch, G. (1980). Do 5-month-olds show object conception in Piaget's sense? *Infant Behavior and Development*, **3**, 265–282.

Miller, D., Cohen, L., & Hill, K. (1970). A methodological investigation of Piaget's theory of object concept development in the sensory-motor period. *Journal of Experimental Child Psychology*, **9**, 59–85.

Moore, M. K. (1973, April). *The genesis of object permanence.* Paper presented at the meeting of the Society for Research in Child Development, Philadelphia.

Moore, M. K., & Meltzoff, A. N. (1978). Imitation, object permanence and language development in infancy: Toward a neo-Piagetian perspective on communicative and cognitive development. In F. D. Minifie & L. L. Lloyd (Eds.), *Communicative and cognitive abilities: Early behavioral assessment.* Baltimore: University Park Press.

Neilson, I. (1982). An alternative explanation of the infant's difficulty in the stage III, IV and V object-concept tasks. *Perception*, **11**, 577–588.

Paradise, E., & Curcio, F. (1974). Relationship of cognitive and affective behaviors to fear of strangers in male infants. *Developmental Psychology*, **10**, 476–483.

Piaget, J. (1954). *The construction of reality in the child* (Mararet Cook, Trans.). New York: Basic. (Original work published 1936)

Presson, C. C., & Ihrig, L. H. (1982). Using mother as a spatial landmark: Evidence against egocentric coding in infancy. *Developmental Psychology*, **18**, 699–703.

Quinton, A. (1973). *The nature of things.* London: Routledge & Kegan Paul.

Rader, N., Spiro, D. J., & Firestone, P. B. (1979). Performance on a stage IV object-permanence task with standard and nonstandard covers. *Child Development*, **50**, 908–910.

Reiser, J. J. (1979). Spatial orientation of six-month-old infants. *Child Development*, **50**, 1078–1087.

Schuberth, R. E., Werner, J. S., & Lipsitt, L. P. (1978). The stage IV error in Piaget's theory of object concept development: A reconsideration of the spatial localization hypothesis. *Child Development*, **49**, 744–748.

Snedecor, G. W., & Cochran, W. G. (1980). *Statistical methods* (7th ed.). Ames: Iowa State University Press.

Sophian, C. (1984). Developing search skills in infancy and early childhood. In C. Sophian (Ed.), *Origins of cognitive skills*. Hillsdale, NJ: Erlbaum.

Sophian, C. (1985). Perseveration and infants' search: A comparison of 2- and 3-location tasks. *Developmental Psychology*, **21**, 187–194.

Sophian, C., & Sage, S. (1983). Developments in infants' search for displaced objects. *Journal of Experimental Child Psychology*, **35**, 143–160.

Sophian, C., & Sage, S. (1985). Infants' search for hidden objects: Developing skills for using information selectively. *Infant Behavior and Development*, **8**, 1–14.

Sophian, C., & Wellman, H. M. (1983). Selective information use and perseveration in the search behavior of infants and young children. *Journal of Experimental Child Psychology*, **35**, 369–390.

Sophian, C., & Yengo, L. (1985). Infants' search for visible objects: Implications for the interpretation of early search errors. *Journal of Experimental Child Psychology*, **40**, 260–278.

Webb, R. A., Massar, B., & Nadolny, R. (1972). Information and strategy in young children's search for hidden objects. *Child Development*, **43**, 91–104.

Wellman, H. M. (Ed.). (1985). *Children's searching: The development of search skill and spatial representation*. Hillsdale, NJ: Erlbaum.

Wellman, H. M., Ritter, K., & Flavell, J. H. (1975). Deliberate memory behavior in the delayed reactions of very young children. *Developmental Psychology*, **11**, 780–787.

Wellman, H. M., & Somerville, S. C. (1982). The development of human search ability. In M. E. Lamb & A. L. Brown (Eds.), *Advances in developmental psychology* (Vol. **2**, pp. 41–84). Hillsdale, NJ: Erlbaum.

Willatts, P. (1979). Adjustment of reaching to change in object position by young infants. *Child Development*, **50**, 911–913.

ACKNOWLEDGMENTS

This research was supported by research grant HD-13317 and by a Research Career Development Award to the first author, both from the National Institute of Child Health and Human Development. An expanded version of this *Monograph,* containing full technical details of the analyses, an expanded report of the findings, and an elaborated discussion, is available from Henry M. Wellman, Center for Human Growth and Development, University of Michigan, 300 North Ingalls Building, 10th Floor, Ann Arbor, MI 48109.

COMMENTARY

BRINGING ORDER TO THE A-NOT-B ERROR

COMMENTARY BY PAUL L. HARRIS

The A-not-B error is a crucial phenomenon for Piaget's account of the development of object permanence. He argued that babies only gradually understand that a hidden object continues to exist quite independent of any actions that might be performed on it. The fact that 9-month-old babies search at an old hiding place (A) even when they have just seen the object moved to a new hiding place (B) appears to provide vivid support for Piaget's claim. The infants act as if they believe that they can re-create the object so long as they simply repeat search actions that have previously led to success. It is not surprising, therefore, that investigators have studied the A-not-B error intensively in the last 15 years, initially to replicate Piaget's findings, but more recently to substantiate alternative interpretations. Latterly, the sheer volume of the research has defied easy synthesis, and investigators have tended to advance explanations around their own findings rather than offering an exhaustive account. Consequently, there has been a danger that research would peter out in the wake of an unwieldy and apparently contradictory set of data.

The great virtue of the *Monograph* by Henry M. Wellman and his colleagues David Cross and Karen Bartsch is that they have restored order to the field. Moreover, the order is simple and compelling. The probability of searching correctly at the new location (B) rather than returning to the old location (A) varies with three independent factors. It increases with age; it declines with the length of the delay between hiding and search; and (to the surprise of Wellman and his colleagues and, indeed, to my own surprise) it increases with the number of hiding places. Other likely variables, by contrast, have little or no effect. For example, the number of times the baby has searched at the old location has no effect; nor, apparently, does the distance between the old and the new containers, whether measured from mid-point to mid-point or from edge to edge. Only one further factor seems to have some influence: correct rather than perseverative search increases if the containers look distinct rather than identical.

We gain this order at some cost. One after another of the recent explanations for the error turn out to be inadequate. Depending on the experimental conditions, we may observe above-chance search at the new correct location or above-chance perseveration at the old location. Therefore, accounts that emphasize only the encoding of the old location (Piaget, 1954) or only the encoding of the new location (Bjork & Cummings, 1984) or that assume some random selection between those two locations when they are identical (Butterworth, 1977; Butterworth, Jarrett, & Hicks, 1982) all fail. Accounts that assume that the infant adopts two distinct and poorly coordinated strategies for search, one leading to A and the other to B, would appear better equipped to explain the pattern of results. Yet, all current two-strategy models also fall short on close examination. In some cases, one or the other of the proposed strategies is inadequate. For example, Gratch, Appel, Evans, LeCompte, & Wright (1987) and Harris (1983, 1987) propose that correct search at B is guided by an easily disrupted immediate motor memory. Such a proposal would not predict correct search at B in the face of longer delays at B or an increase in the number of hiding places. Diamond (1985) attributes perseveration at A to a motor habit and would therefore predict that it should increase with the number of previous search actions at A, a prediction that is in no way supported by the meta-analysis. Other accounts fail because, although the strategies themselves are acceptable, investigators fail to give an adequate account of how the infant selects between them. Sophian and Wellman (1983), for example, do not explain how an increase in the number of hiding places could tilt selection toward the new hiding place at B. Horobin and Acredolo (1986) point out that increasing the distance of B from A, which typically happens when more hiding places are inserted between them, might make B more discriminable from A, but the meta-analysis appears to provide no support for the claim that distance plays a causal role.

Faced with such orderly findings and no adequate explanation, Wellman and his colleagues offer a new alternative. They start by identifying two search strategies: a direct-finding approach and an inferred-location approach. Direct finding, as its name implies, is guided by the most recent visible information about the direction in which an object has disappeared. Thus, if an object has just been seen disappearing under cloth B, the direct-finding approach prompts the child to search at B. Wellman and his colleagues do not say so explicitly, but one may conclude that this strategy relies on some memory for the direction of disappearance. This is necessarily the case because search is initiated after the visible movement that results in the occlusion of the object has terminated; thus, there is no visible information to guide search at the moment when it is initiated. The second of the two strategies—the inferred-location approach—is quite novel. As Wellman and his colleagues point out, some objects do not stay put at the point of disappearance; they move on to a new location. Thus, borrowing the two examples used by Wellman and his colleagues, a dog may disappear at one location and move on to a second, and a ball may roll under the front of the couch and continue rolling to the back of the couch. A sensible strategy under these circumstances is to extrapolate beyond the point of disappearance, in the direction of disappearance, and to search at some accessible point along the inferred trajectory, be it the next-door neighbor's house or the back of the couch.

Obviously, both the direct-finding and the inferred-location strategy are useful depending on the circumstances. Wellman and his colleagues suggest that infants who commit the A-not-B error have both strategies available but do not know when to use one rather than the other. On B trials, adoption of the direct-finding approach will lead to correct search. Perseverative errors to A, however, occur when the infant makes use of the inferred-location approach rather than relying on the direct-finding approach. This is more likely to happen when a delay is imposed or when the containers are identical. Each of these conditions prompts the infant to reflect and inhibits the immediate direct-finding approach, thereby increasing the likelihood of the inferred-location strategy.

This account is an improvement over earlier proposals in that it identifies two fairly robust strategies that might lead to systematically correct search or to systematic perseveration. However, I have considerable reservations about the inferred-location strategy and also about the way in which selection between them is supposed to occur.

The first problem is that the two examples provided by Wellman and his colleagues of the inferred-location approach need to be fudged if they are to be applied to perseverative search at A. The essence of the two examples is that the observer anticipates some future location on the basis of the direction of travel at the moment of disappearance. This is especially clear in the case of the ball rolling under the couch. Dogs, admittedly, do not travel in straight lines, but even they may head off on some particular route. Construing the examples in this fashion leads to two difficulties. There is some evidence that young infants can reach out and catch an object moving along a visible trajectory (von Hofsten, 1983) and can even interpolate an invisible trajectory (Baillargeon, 1986), but there is little evidence that infants can search manually at some point along an interpolated trajectory at 8 or 9 months. Infants of that age can learn to gaze toward the far side of a screen when an object that moves behind it regularly reappears there, but this visual search builds up over trials and is not shown on initial trials

(Nelson, 1971); moreover, it involves visual tracking only rather than manual retrieval. The second difficulty is that, even were such a capacity for extrapolation plus manual search identified, thereby lending credence to the availability of the inferred-location strategy, its relevance to perseveration would be tenuous. Neither a strategy of extrapolation nor the two examples used by Wellman and his colleagues suggest in any way how the inferred location might turn out to be some location that the object occupied *prior* to its disappearance. They suggest, instead, that the inferred location will turn out to be some location that the object might move to *after* its disappearance. Yet, according to Wellman and his colleagues, the adoption of the inferred-location approach leads infants to return to an old location, not to approach a new one.

Conceivably, Wellman and his colleagues intend the dog and the ball examples to illustrate only the kind of problem that infants might encounter, not the type of strategy that they adopt. Thus, adults and older children might extrapolate an invisible trajectory in appropriate circumstances, but infants do not. Faced with objects that move after they disappear, infants might discover that the direct-finding approach fails and, lacking any insight into invisible movement, go back to a previous hiding place in the hope of finding the object there. Presumably, this strategy would sometimes lead to success because objects may return invisibly to an earlier location. For example, the dog may disappear but end up going home; the ball may roll under the couch and keep on rolling into the toy cupboard. In each of these cases, search at an old location would be successful. Thus, the strategy of returning to an old location, having occasionally been crowned with success, might be overextended to cases in which the object moves to a new hiding place and stays there.

Even with this alternative gloss, however, there still remain difficulties with the selection procedure. Recall that Wellman and his colleagues think of the inferred-location approach as the more reflective approach, one that is prompted by a delay. This offers a reasonable explanation of the fact that perseverative error is more likely when a delay is imposed. However, from the work of Diamond (1985) and from the results of the meta-analysis itself, we also know that older infants can tolerate longer delays than can younger infants. The only way to interpret this result in the light of the postulates made by Wellman and his colleagues is to suppose that older infants take *longer* to initiate reflection, so that, even with longer delays, they do not shift to the error-prone inferred-location strategy. This clearly makes little sense. One might surely expect that older infants would be faster to initiate reflection. In this case, they would require shorter delays before shifting to the indirect strategy, a prediction that is obviously not borne out by the meta-analysis. This argument illustrates a more general point: whatever postulate we make to explain the switch from a B approach to an A approach, it must invoke some process that can plausibly lead to a postponement of the switch with age. That is why it is reasonable to assume that the information that mediates search at B becomes weaker over time. The finding that older infants can tolerate longer delays is then easily explained by assuming that the weakening of that information proceeds more slowly in the older infant. Equally, that same line of interpretation can explain why distinctiveness is a protective factor. The more distinctive the information that mediates search at B, the more likely it is to withstand the attenuating effects of delay.

Wellman and his colleagues also use their account to explain why accuracy increases rather than declines when extra hiding locations are introduced. They argue that the presence of many locations "makes it more difficult for the infant to conceive of the B-trial hiding as an extension in time and space of A-trial occurrences" (p. 43) and that, therefore, the inferred-location strategy is never attempted. I find this explanation unconvincing. Instead, one could reasonably speculate that the presence of so many intermediate locations all identical to the B location would inhibit the direct-finding approach or that so many alternatives would prompt more reflection, increasing the likelihood of the inferred-location approach.

Aside from these interpretive problems, the finding that an increase in the number of locations increases accurate search at B deserves some further comment. As I noted earlier, this is a striking result. If it turns out to be a robust finding, not only will the meta-analysis have brought order to previously explored variables such as delay and the number of hidings, but it will also have revealed the potency of a variable that was introduced chiefly for methodological reasons (cf. Bjork & Cummings, 1984). Is it likely to be a robust finding? Here, I must acknowledge some doubts. First, it emerges only in the meta-analysis itself. When we examine individual studies in which the effect of the number of locations has been assessed (Bjork & Cummings, 1984; Sophian, 1985), there is no indication that search at B is more accurate with more hiding places. Indeed, when the distance between A and B is held constant, the insertion of additional hiding places between A and B tends to reduce accuracy. Thus, when we compare the wide-pair condition with the six-location condition from Horobin and Acredolo (1986), we find that search is more accurate in the wide-pair condition. On the other hand, this condition repeatedly emerges as an outlier in the meta-analysis. For example, it emerged as an outlier in the analysis of perseverative error in standard two-location tasks (p. 14), in omnibus two-location tasks (p. 18), and in standard multilocation tasks (p. 21). It also emerged as an outlier in the analysis of correct search in standard multilocation tasks (p. 24). Finally, it emerged in the analysis of distance and distinctiveness (p. 28). Two other studies (included only in the omnibus analysis of two-location tasks) also emerge as outliers—Butterworth (1975, Experiment 1) and Harris (1973, Experiment 3).

Outliers are important because they suggest that some variable is at work that has not been included in the meta-analysis. Is it possible to find a common thread among the three outliers? At first sight, this seems unlikely because each appears to introduce some idiosyncratic variation. Thus, Butterworth (1975) put the A location in a central position and the B location to one side and observed a decrease in perseveration. Harris (1973) lowered the curtain at hiding-place A only after the curtain at hiding-place B had been lowered and observed an increase in perseveration. Horobin and Acredolo (1986) separated the edges of the A and the B containers by over 41 cm (more than any comparable study) and observed a decrease in perseveration. These disparate findings do not appear to reflect some common underlying process. Still, with two plausible assumptions, we can explain each of them. Let us suppose that the infant's memory for the B location is quite short lived, albeit increasingly robust with age. That memory serves to fix the baby's visual attention on the B location and can even draw it back to the B location after a brief glance elsewhere. Various factors will influence the likelihood that the baby is gazing at B and will search there when the opportunity to search arises. Distractions in the periphery will reduce it; assuming that the baby's gaze is typically directed toward the mid-line, the placement of B at the mid-line will increase it. The three outliers now fall into place. Butterworth (1975) observed a reduction in perseveration when B was at the mid-line—the infant's likely direction of gaze—rather than at the periphery. Harris (1973) observed an increase in perseveration when a distraction in the periphery was introduced immediately prior to the opportunity to search. Horobin and Acredolo (1986) observed a reduction in perseveration when the edge of the A container may well have been close to the edge of the infant's peripheral visual field, effectively creating a single-location task.

I have mentioned these assumptions because they form part of an account that, in my view, can capture all the findings of the meta-analysis, including those that emerge from the outlying studies identified above. This account leans heavily on ideas that I have proposed elsewhere (Harris, in press). Like Wellman and his colleagues, I believe that there are two search modes, one leading the infant to search at A and the other leading the infant to search at B. Search at B depends on the likelihood of the baby gazing at B at the moment of search. Whether the baby gazes at B at the moment of search depends in turn on the availability in short-term memory of information about the direction in which the object disappeared. The duration of that short-term memory increases with age, allowing the baby to shift its gaze during the delay period but to refixate B at the moment of search. These assumptions lead naturally to the prediction that correct search at B is more likely among infants who have continuously fixated B throughout any delay period (Cornell, 1979; Diamond, 1985; Horobin & Acredolo, 1986).

Nevertheless, the crucial information in memory is not motoric or kinesthetic but visual. The baby can, in principle, change its posture or direction of gaze and still search at B correctly, so long as memory about the direction of disappearance of the object is still available in short-term memory to draw the infant's gaze back to B. Thus, even if the fixation of the infant is distracted away from B, search can be accurate across a short delay among younger infants and across a longer delay among older infants (Diamond, 1985). It is also important to note that all the above assumptions can be readily extended to search on A trials, as I indicate below.

In many respects, these assumptions are similar to those made by Wellman and his colleagues for the direct-finding approach. Nevertheless, they spell out the relation between age, duration of immediate memory, and direction of gaze in more detail, thereby leading to a more concrete and testable explanation of how older infants tolerate longer delays.

The infant does have a second search strategy available, and, on B trials, this can sometimes lead to search at A. This second strategy relies on memory for landmark information in the following way. Once an object has been found at a particular landmark such as a cover, the location and identity of that landmark are entered into long-term memory, and that stored information can guide search. It endures across trials rather than fading within a few seconds of the object's disappearance. An infant whose memory for the direction of disappearance of the object is weak or nonexistent will be less likely to gaze at B just prior to search, more likely to gaze at the landmark where the object was found on previous trials, more likely to be reminded of those previous trials, and, hence, more likely to search there. There is considerable evidence that infants of 8 or 9 months can note and remember landmarks to guide their direction of gaze or search (Harris, 1983). Note that this search strategy is not as sophisticated as the inferred-location approach postulated by Wellman and his colleagues, but it has more evidence to support it.

The above assumptions can readily explain accurate search on A trials. On the initial A trial, the landmark code does not exist since the object has not yet been found at A, but the infant can rely on the short-term code at least over short intervals. On subsequent A trials, both short- and long-term memory information orient the baby toward accurate search at A.

Selection between the two strategies on B trials is not based on any conceptual insight into the fact that the most recent direction of disappearance should lead to the elimination of previous locations of reappearance as potential current locations for the object since the baby does not appreciate that only a single object is involved, necessarily located at a single place (Harris, 1983, 1987). Instead, selection is governed by factors that influence the infant's direction of gaze just prior to search. Among those factors, delay is an especially important variable since it influences the availability of information about the direction in which the object disappeared; but other factors, such as the salience of A in the infant's peripheral field or whether the baby encounters an obstacle at B and turns away in frustration (Harris, 1974), can also play a role.

There is one outstanding problem. The meta-analysis strongly suggests that an increase in the number of locations increases correct search at B. Does the alternative account that I have proposed offer a convincing explanation of that finding? It does not. It does predict that, when the landmark A is placed outside the baby's effective visual field, the probability of perseveration to A will be reduced. It also predicts that landmarks similar to A might attract search (particularly if they are placed between A and B and are easily noticed), thereby reducing the likelihood of perseveration to A. What it does not predict is that the mere presence of more containers positioned between A and B will lead the infant to search more accurately at B.

There is, however, an alternative way to interpret the results of the meta-analysis. Let us suppose that the distance between the A and the B containers in a two-location task has little effect until the distance between A and B exceeds the infant's effective visual field. This explains why edge-to-edge distance has little effect when it is varied within certain limits but produces an anomalous drop in error when that limit is exceeded (as indexed by the wide-pair condition of Horobin & Acredolo, 1986). An increase in the number of containers will sometimes mimic the wide-pair effect, but not always. It is especially likely to occur when there are five or six rather than two or three hiding places and when A and B are at either end of a linear or semicircular arrangement. Pooling studies with the number of locations varying from two to six would create the impression that number of locations was the crucial variable rather than the wide-pair effect. Thus, the alternative account that I have advanced cannot explain the number of locations effect, but it does offer a straightforward explanation of the wide-pair effect. Indeed, it predicts that an increase in the number of locations interposed between A and B will not increase correct search at B so long as the distance between A and B remains constant. If anything, the intermediate locations will draw search away from B. To my knowledge, there is no experimental study that runs counter to this prediction, but future research may produce one.

I am very grateful to Wellman and his colleagues for carrying out the meta-analysis, yet I have had the temerity to offer a different account from theirs. Does that imply that, despite the clear results of the meta-analysis, the study of infant search will continue to be fraught with disagreement? I think that would be a superficial conclusion. It is important to note several important similarities between the two accounts. Each postulates two distinct modes of search. Each invokes some kind of switching mechanism by means of which the strategy leading to search at B is replaced by the strategy leading to search at A. Each assumes that delay increases the likelihood of that switch being activated. Future research may well cast doubt on the specific proposals contained in each account concerning the exact nature of the two components and the switching mechanism. The general notion of two combined components plus a switching mechanism, on the other hand, is likely to prove very durable. The meta-analysis provides compelling arguments for exactly that approach. It is a major achievement, and it will provide, I hope, a stable backdrop against which investigators can continue to debate.

References

Baillargeon, R. (1986). Representing the existence and the location of hidden objects: Object permanence in six- and eight-month-old infants. *Cognition, 23,* 21–41.

Bjork, E. L., & Cummings, E. M. (1984). Infant search errors: Stage of concept development or stage of memory development. *Memory and Cognition, 12*(1), 1–19.

Butterworth, G. E. (1975). Object identity in infancy: The interaction of spatial location codes in determining search errors. *Child Development, 46,* 866–870.

Butterworth, G. E. (1977). Object disappearance and error in Piaget's stage IV task. *Journal of Experimental Child Psychology, 23,* 391–401.

Butterworth, G. E., Jarrett, N., & Hicks, L. (1982). Spatio-temporal identity in infancy: Perceptual competence or conceptual deficit? *Developmental Psychology, 18,* 435–449.

Cornell, E. H. (1979). The effects of cue distinctiveness on infant's manual search. *Journal of Experimental Child Psychology, 32,* 330–342.

Diamond, A. (1985). Development of the ability to use recall to guide action as indicated by infant's performance on AB. *Child Development, 56,* 868–883.

Gratch, G., Appel, K. J., Evans, W. F., LeCompte, G. K., & Wright, N. A. (1974). Piaget's stage IV object concept error: Evidence of forgetting or object conception. *Child Development, 45,* 71–77.

Harris, P. L. (1973). Perseverative errors in search by young infants. *Child Development, 44,* 28–33.

Harris, P. L. (1974). Perseverative search at a visibly empty place by young infants. *Journal of Experimental Child Psychology, 18,* 535–542.

Harris, P. L. (1983). Infant cognition. In M. M. Haith & J. J. Campos (Eds.), P. H. Mussen (Series Ed.), *Handbook of child psychology: Vol. 2. Infancy and developmental psychobiology* (pp. 689–782). New York: Wiley.

Harris, P. L. (1987). The development of search. In P. Salapatek & L. B. Cohen (Eds.), *Handbook of infant perception* (Vol. 2, pp. 155–207). New York: Academic Press.

Harris, P. L. (in press). The development of object permanence. In A. Slater & J. G. Bremner (Eds.), *The psychology of infancy.* Hillsdale, N.J.: Erlbaum.

Horobin, K. M., & Acredolo, L. P. (1986). The role of attentiveness, mobility history, and separation of hiding sites on stage IV search behavior. *Journal of Experimental Child Psychology, 41,* 114–127.

Nelson, K. E. (1971). Accommodation of visual tracking patterns in human infants to object movement patterns. *Journal of Experimental Child Psychology, 12,* 182–196.

Piaget, J. (1954). *The construction of reality in the child.* New York: Basic.

Sophian, C. (1985). Perseveration and infant's search: A comparison of 2- and 3-location tasks. *Developmental Psychology, 21,* 187–194.

Sophian, C., & Wellman, H. M. (1983). Selective information use and perseveration in the search behavior of infants and young children. *Journal of Experimental Child Psychology,* **35,** 369–390.

von Hofsten, C. (1983). Catching skills in infancy. *Journal of Experimental Psychology: Human Perception and Performance,* **9,** 75–87.

[**Paul L. Harris** (D.Phil. 1971, Oxford University) is university lecturer in the Department of Experimental Psychology and fellow of St. John's College, Oxford University. Recent works include Infant cognition, in M. M. Haith & J. J. Campos (Eds.), P. H. Mussen (Series Ed.), *Handbook of child psychology: Vol 2. Infancy and developmental psychobiology* (1983); and The development of search, in P. Salapatek & L. B. Cohen (Eds.), *Handbook of infant perception* (Vol. 2) (1987). His research area is cognitive development, especially the child's concept of mind.]

MORE DATA, MORE THEORY, AND MORE ORDER

REPLY BY THE AUTHORS

To serve up a helping of clarity and order from a potentially chaotic data base and to set the table for informed theoretical debate about an important developmental acquisition were the primary goals of our meta-analysis. It is cheering, therefore, to be described as having accomplished these aims. Of course, Harris has more to say than this, and so do we. In what follows, we try to avoid providing commentary on Harris's commentary; that raises the specter of an infinite regression. Instead, our aim is to add some further clarity and analyses; Harris's comments have caused us to do some additional work.

Robustness

Like any empirical endeavor, meta-analytic findings may not stand the test of time. Sensibly, Harris raises this question of the robustness of our findings. In its most general form, the question is, If new findings were included, would the same conclusions obtain? Such additional findings may come from new research or from prior research not included in the analyses.

No meta-analyst can guarantee to have included all the pertinent studies and conditions, overlooking none. One can aim only to include most of the literature and try to ensure that the picture obtained is representative. We can test directly whether our findings are robust in this sense because we failed to include an article by Freeman, Lloyd, and Sinha (1980) in our original data base. In a series of studies, they present nine different A-not-B conditions suitable for our omnibus two-location analysis. Since our sample for that analysis included 55 conditions, nine new conditions constitutes a nontrivial addition. Consequently, we reconducted the omnibus two-location analysis, including the conditions of Freeman et al., for a total of 64 data points. This updated analysis replicates the original analysis in all details. Thus, in the regression of age, delay, A trials, and year of publication on perseverative errors, age, $F(1,62) = 18.27, p < .001$, and delay, $F(1,61) = 13.96, p < .001$, were once again important carriers in the regression, while A trials, $F(1,60) = 1.82$, and year, $F < 1$, matter little. If only age and delay are used in the linear model for errors, $R^2 = .40$, whereas $R^2 = .41$ in the original analysis.

To be clear, Harris does not doubt the robustness of most of our core findings. His objection is more specific than that. But the specific case inspires the general question. This updated analysis thus provides comforting support for the strength of our original findings.

Harris's specific concern is that the number of locations effect, apparent in the multilocation analysis, may not be robust. We found that, as the number of locations available increases, correct search increases. Here, our data base is smaller (only 24 conditions have used more than two locations), and we have no additional conditions to analyze to bolster confidence in our original analysis. The effect deserves further research. However, Harris's contention that, "when we examine individual studies in which the effect of the number of locations has been assessed . . . , there is no indication that search at B is more accurate with more hiding places" (p. 56) seems misleading. Using our transformed measure of correct search (Z correct, which takes into account the total number of incorrect locations that the infant could potentially search), Bjork and Cummings (1984) found $-.12$ versus .45 correct searching for two versus five locations, respectively; Sophian (1985) found .06 versus .19 correct searching for two versus three locations, respectively; and Horobin and Acredolo (1986) found .14, .78, and .95 correct searching for their two-location close, two-location wide, and six-location conditions, respectively. With this scoring, zero represents random searching, and increasingly positive scores indicate increasingly nonrandom, correct responding. The levels of these scores vary across studies since the delays, ages, and exact number of locations differ across studies. Nonetheless, the within-study comparisons do corroborate the meta-analytic finding that increasing the number of locations is consistently related to increased correct searching.

Finally, Harris suggests that Horobin and Acredolo's (1986) "outlying" wide-pair results can be explained by a visual field interpretation. If the two containers are so far apart that, when the infant looks at one, the other is not even in his or her visual field, then he or she is faced with a simple single-location search problem and, thus, searches correctly. This explanation seems quite plausible. But Harris goes on to suggest that this wide-pair effect could produce the number of locations effect obtained in the meta-analysis. In general, this seems implausible because, if a visual field effect accounts for the number of locations effect, then it is not something peculiar to Horobin and Acredolo's condition and, hence, does not seem to explain that condition's status as an outlier. More specifically, Harris proposes that, when a great many locations are used—five or six—this could directly produce the wide-pair effect and, thus, indirectly produce the number of locations effect. Note that, by this reasoning, the number of locations effect itself should be due essentially to increased correct searching given quite large numbers of locations—five or six. That is, in the pooled data, there should be a notable jump or acceleration in correct searching specific to using a great many locations (and thereby exceeding the infant's visual field). How-ever, the effect of number of locations is regular and linear, and, if any-thing, it tapers off a bit as more and more locations are added. In the multilocations analysis, the proportion of correct searching is .48 ($N = 24$) on two-location tasks, .54 ($N = 16$) on three-location tasks, .63 ($N = 6$) on five-location tasks, and .57 ($N = 2$) on six-location tasks.

In general, then, further analyses continue to support the robustness of our basic findings. Moreover, with respect to the number of locations effect, both within-study and across-study analyses continue to support the exis-tence and importance of that finding.

Theoretical Interpretations

The above comments speak to the general empirical findings of the analyses. In addition to documenting these findings, we advanced a theoreti-cal interpretation. Harris raises some doubts about our proposal and offers an alternative. One thing that Harris's comments help make clear is that both his account and our account fit the data well in many ways but are strained with respect to one or another of the findings. With respect to his account, Harris admits that "the alternative account that I have advanced cannot explain the number of locations effect" (p. 59). As noted above, we believe this effect is important and robust, despite Harris's thoughtful ef-forts to make it disappear.

With respect to our account, Harris is correct that it does not provide a straightforward interpretation of how delay influences search with increas-ing age. Our interpretation here is not detailed in the *Monograph*. However, we did say in several places that we felt that the meta-analysis provides primarily a picture of 9-month-old search coupled with a straightforward finding that search becomes more correct with increasing age. It does not provide a good description of how factors such as delay and number of locations interact with increasing age. With this as background, we feel that two things happen with increasing age—infants get more reflective, and, thus, an inferred-location approach becomes more prevalent. But, in addition, infants get more inferentially accurate. That is, they change from making an incorrect inference (the item is at A) to making a correct one (the item is at B). Hence, less lengthy delays can invoke an inferred-location approach as infants get older, and older children can still be increasingly correct. This interpretation requires a test involving further research with infants across a range of ages. As noted in the *Monograph*, the field could benefit more generally from such truly developmental data.

Harris also articulates some doubts about the general nature and plausibility of our inferred-location approach. Most important, he does not see how such an approach could induce infants to consider the objects' location at a prior time and place; rather it should lead them to extrapolate its future trajectory. Here, our own admittedly limited set of examples has clouded the issue, so we welcome the opportunity to clarify and amplify. First, even in the two examples that Harris refers to, consideration of future locales is based on extrapolation. Extrapolation involves considering the history of the object's movement up until its disappearance. Extrapolation is thus backward looking, in this sense of attending to a history of movements in order to infer a future trajectory. Our general point is that, in attending to such prior information at all, the infant may falsely conceive of the object as residing at a prior locale.

However, there is a better set of examples that we should have stressed more in our presentation. An infant who has to search for an object on B trials of an A-then-B task faces a situation very similar to one we all face when having to search for a lost object. Suppose I discover that my glasses are lost. I often try to recall where I last had them and then, beginning there, re-search my itinerary since then. Our contention is simply that, in the A-then-B task, young infants do something like this, then incorrectly interpret and rely on the information about past possession and, consequently, search at A first rather than at B. It is this sort of faulty inferred-location reasoning that we claim underlies infant's perseverative searching. This is why we suggest that A-not-B errors are the incorrect antecedents of the sort of correct searching demonstrated by Haake and Somerville (1985) in 15-month-olds.

Finally, a meta-analytic pooling of the data bears on Harris's alternative account. Harris's new account is essentially a memory account as we described that class of proposals in the *Monograph*. His contention is that memory for the B information takes the form of a short-term code that decays rapidly unless bolstered by gazing to B. Memory for the A information, in contrast, takes the form of a long-term code. Thus, after a suitable delay on B trials (in the absence of direct gazing to B), infants are left with only A information and, consequently, search at A. As we noted in our discussion of overlearning, primacy, and proactive interference, such an account must propose a basis for why memories for the A and B information are different. Harris's proposal is that, at the point in the initial B trial at which the infant must search for the object, A information is coded differently from B information. This is because, on the A trial, the object has been hidden *and* has been found but, on the B-trial, the infant has as yet witnessed only a hiding.

To be convincing, Harris's account must go beyond simply asserting that A experience results in a long-term code and that B experience results in a short-term one. He must specify why A experience causes such a result but B experience does not. Here, Harris is unclear. He does say that the A-trial experience has special force because the "object has been found" (p. 58), but how does that work? One plausible possibility is that, on A trials, the infant has actively found the object, actively consolidating the A information into a long-term code. Unfortunately, actively finding the object does not have the predicted effect.

Two studies have compared A-trial conditions in which infants actively found the hidden object with passive conditions in which they merely saw someone else hide and retrieve the object at A (Evans, 1973; Sophian & Wellman, 1983). If active finding establishes the long-term representation proposed by Harris, then this difference in A-trial experience should influence perseveration significantly. It does not. Evans conducted two different comparisons between passive and active A experiences. In both cases, six of the 12 infants perseverated with passive experience, and seven of the 12 did so with active experience. Sophian and Wellman included a similar comparison. Passive experience produced 31% perseverative searching, and active experience produced 31% perseverative searching.

An alternative possibility is that an A-trial experience of witnessing a hiding and witnessing (or actively producing) a finding constitutes two pieces of information connecting the object's location to A. In contrast, simply witnessing a disappearance at B produces a single such connection. Thus, a sufficient number of connections of the object and a location might be needed to establish a long-term code. More generally, since Harris's proposal focuses on the special benefit of having found the object at A, then, regardless of the specific long-term memory-consolidation mechanism proposed, increased experience of finding the object at A could be expected to establish increasingly the requisite long-term encoding of information. But here the meta-analysis is quite clear. Increasing the number of A trials has no such effect; it does not produce increased perseveration. The absence of an A-trial effect is not necessarily fatal to Harris's account, but it certainly seems uncongenial.

Our point is not that our proposal is right and that Harris's is wrong. Both are post hoc and probably destined to prove inadequate. Our point is to demonstrate once again the utility of a comprehensive consideration of all the findings pooled across studies. The findings do present an orderly pattern of phenomena ripe for creative theory building but appropriately constraining. On this, Harris and we most certainly agree.

We want to end on another point of agreement, namely, the importance of the phenomena addressed by studies of infant searching and, thus, the importance of the data and the theories. As should now be clear, searching for objects requires both a basic conceptual achievement and a rudimentary problem-solving repertoire: knowing that objects exist in an encompassing space including both self and object even when hidden from view and an ability to represent an as-yet unattained goal and to adopt some specific course of action aimed at attaining it. Studies of infant searching yield data about the ontogenesis of both these basic abilities. In addition, they provide insight on how conceptual knowledge and problem-solving skill influence and constrain one another. Getting the data right and getting the theoretical explanations right are thus matters of considerable importance for our understanding of early cognitive development.

References

Bjork, E. L., & Cummings, E. M. (1984). Infant search errors: Stage of concept development or stage of memory development. *Memory and Cognition*, **12**, 1–19.

Evans, W. F. (1973). *The stage IV error in Piaget's theory of object concept development: An investigation of the role of activity.* Unpublished dissertation proposal, University of Houston.

Haake, R. J., & Somerville, S. C. (1985). Development of logical search in infancy. *Developmental Psychology*, **21**, 176–186.

Horobin, K. M., & Acredolo, L. P. (1986). The role of attentiveness, mobility history, and separation of hiding sites on stage IV search behavior. *Journal of Experimental Child Psychology*, **41**, 114–127.

Freeman, N. H., Lloyd, S., & Sinha, C. G. (1980). Infant search tasks reveal early concepts of containment and canonical usage of objects. *Cognition*, **8**, 243–262.

Sophian, C. (1985). Perseveration and infants' search: A comparison of 2- and 3-location tasks. *Developmental Psychology*, **21**, 187–194.

Sophian, C., & Wellman, H. M. (1983). Selective information use and perseveration in the search behavior of infants and young children. *Journal of Experimental Child Psychology*, **35**, 369–390.

MONOGRAPHS

OF THE SOCIETY FOR RESEARCH IN CHILD DEVELOPMENT

VOLUME 51, 1986

PUBLISHED BY THE UNIVERSITY OF CHICAGO PRESS FOR THE

SOCIETY FOR RESEARCH IN CHILD DEVELOPMENT

VOLUME 51, NUMBERS 1–3

© 1986–1987 by the Society for Research in Child Development, Inc.

All rights reserved.

PUBLISHED BY THE UNIVERSITY OF CHICAGO PRESS
CHICAGO, ILLINOIS, U.S.A.

MONOGRAPHS OF THE SOCIETY FOR RESEARCH IN CHILD DEVELOPMENT

VOLUME 51, 1986

No. 1   JOHN H. FLAVELL, FRANCES L. GREEN, and ELEANOR R. FLAVELL. Development of Knowledge about the Appearance-Reality Distinction. With Commentaries by MALCOLM W. WATSON and JOSEPH C. CAMPIONE. Pp. v + 89 (Serial No. 212).

No. 2   KENNETH A. DODGE, GREGORY S. PETTIT, CYNTHIA L. McCLASKEY, and MELISSA M. BROWN. Social Competence in Children. With Commentary by JOHN M. GOTTMAN. Pp. vi + 85 (Serial No. 213).

No. 3   HENRY M. WELLMAN, DAVID CROSS, and KAREN BARTSCH. Infant Search and Object Permanence: A Meta-Analysis of the A-Not-B Error. With Commentary by PAUL L. HARRIS. Pp. vi + 67 (Serial No. 214).